THE SPENDER'S GUIDE TO

Debt-Free Living

HOW A *Spending Fast*
HELPED ME GET FROM
Broke to Badass
IN RECORD TIME

THE SPENDER'S GUIDE TO
Debt-Free Living

ANNA NEWELL JONES

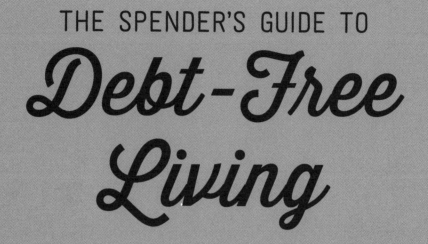

WILLIAM MORROW

An Imprint of HarperCollins*Publishers*

THE SPENDER'S GUIDE TO DEBT-FREE LIVING. Copyright © 2016 by Anna Newell Jones. All rights reserved. Printed in the United States of America. No part of this book may be used or reproduced in any manner whatsoever without written permission except in the case of brief quotations embodied in critical articles and reviews. For information address HarperCollins Publishers, 195 Broadway, New York, NY 10007.

HarperCollins books may be purchased for educational, business, or sales promotional use. For information please e-mail the Special Markets Department at SPsales@harpercollins.com.

FIRST EDITION

Designed by Diahann Sturge

Illustrations by Tuesday Bassen

Library of Congress Cataloging-in-Publication Data has been applied for.

ISBN 978-0-06-236718-1

16 17 18 19 20 OV/RRD 10 9 8 7 6 5 4 3 2 1

For my guys, Aaron and Henry,
and for every person who has ever had the courage
to trust their gut and live the life they were meant to.

CONTENTS

THE SPENDER'S GUIDE TO

INTRODUCTION:
CAN A SPENDER *REALLY* LIVE DEBT-FREE?

A few years ago I realized I was stuck in a bad pattern. Often I would find myself telling everyone I owed money to that there just wasn't any left after the bills were paid. Even though I always had the cutest clothes and latest gadgets, I was living paycheck to paycheck. And, despite working more than forty hours a week, I had nothing left to pay back the debts that constantly hung overhead. Deep down, though, I knew the truth. I knew that while I was having a hard time paying back the money I owed to others, when it came down to it, I was *always* able to find money when I wanted something. I told myself that I didn't want to spend the way I did but, really, who was I kidding? I liked it. And I still like spending money, I like new things. I love unique, one-of-a-kind, quirky things. I live for finding that perfect shirt, or decoration for my house. You see, I'm a Spender. I love the hunt. I love the excitement of finding that item I've been looking everywhere for. Adrenaline flows through me, and I happily hand over my money. Me, a self-proclaimed "Natural Spender" who came out of the womb with a buck burning a hole in my pocket ever living debt-free? Not likely. I knew that since I couldn't budget, a debt-free life was not in the cards for me. I knew that if budgeting had anything to do with living debt-free I was totally screwed. Plus, I had halfheartedly tried at least a dozen different methods to try to get my act together. After each failed attempt, I'd tell myself that next month would be The Month that I'd finally be able to nail down this "spending too much" issue and I'd *finally* get the debt under control. But that next month was always just outside of my grip. "Getting things under control" was elusive. I wanted to find a way to rein in my finances, but the solution I was seeking had to be extremely effective and keep me motivated. It also had to be simple and straightforward. I could never find the right getting-out-of-debt combo—until I did.

When I wrote my very first blog post for my website, AndThenWeSaved.com, I was casually sharing about this semicrazy idea that I had: I would go an entire year spending money only on necessities, just to see what would happen. I wanted to see if I could take on a challenge like that. Sure, I wanted to believe I could go a whole year without spending on anything but needs, but I was the biggest skeptic of all. I knew myself. I knew how much I loved to spend money. I thought that maybe if I went public about my debt and about how much it weighed on me, I'd be more likely to stick to the plan and not immediately ditch the entire idea once things got difficult. When I put myself out there, when I made myself vulnerable, and when I started to share the dirty, honest details about my debt on my website, something amazing happened. While the shame I felt about getting myself into a big financial mess didn't instantly disappear, I quickly learned that I wasn't the only one struggling to find a way to get out of debt that would actually work. Turns out that other people had trouble following a budget too. Some people were also spending money on crazy things, as I had been doing. And while the readers of my blog were coming from different backgrounds and were coping with different situations, the universal theme was that we all felt hopeless and ashamed of the messes we had gotten into with our spending. We all wanted, and desperately needed, a way out that would work—and quickly. I will always be grateful to the people who shared, and continue to share, their stories with me:

> "Unplanned expenses keep popping up. Medical bills, car repairs, friends' weddings, baby showers, and so on."
>
> "I just don't make enough money."
>
> "I sit at a desk in a very stressful job. Shopping online makes me feel better, so I spend money instead of saving and paying down debt."

It was helpful to know that I wasn't the only person who felt out of control with my finances. But another commonality appeared from the e-mails I was receiving from readers. People were getting motivated by my experience and started asking me for help with *their* Spending Fasts, a year-long period of spending money only on what is absolutely needed. That's when I realized that people were relying on me. They were actually coming *to me* for solutions. It turns out that they too had been tormented by the loud, constant swirling chatter of thoughts: *But I want it. I deserve it. It's such a good deal! It's so cute! It's perfect! It's not that expensive.* Many of my readers also felt so crippled by their debt that they didn't see a way out. The debt had become all-consuming. Some even felt they would die in debt. It turns out that this is a pretty common feeling today. According to a survey by creditcards.com, *nearly one in five consumers with loans said they think they will never be able to finish paying off their debt.*

That's a pretty grim feeling, and there was definitely a time when I didn't think getting out of debt could be real for me, either. And that's why my blog and this book exist—because it is possible to get out of debt, and it can be done very quickly. I want to help you picture a life without debt, shame, worry, and anxiety. The feel-like-shit cycle can end right here, right now. It's hard work, and it can be easy to take the view that getting out of debt and spending money "normally" just won't happen. But it can! As you'll soon see, I learned there is a sweet spot between "Spend All the Money!" and "Spend No Money!"

For me, getting out of debt was about having choices: not having to take a job I despise simply because I needed the paycheck, and being able to spend my money on things that are important to me. I wanted my financial life to be about more than just covering my minimum balance each month or not bouncing a check. There are so many reasons that making the sacrifices to get out of debt are worth it, and I'm grateful that my readers shared their thoughts on this topic. They all said it was worth it because:

> "I want to work less and travel!"
> "It's affecting the decisions I want to make."
> "My debt is weighing me down."
> "I want my money to go toward things that help me reach my goals and my dreams."
> "I want to get married and have a family someday."
> "I'm sick of skimping on life because I'm spending $600 a month on credit card payments."
> "I want to be able to retire."
> "I don't want to have to worry about the future."

Whatever makes getting out of debt worth it *to you*, know you can get there. I wrote this book because I'm a regular person, just like you. I'm not a personal finance legend like Robert Kiyosaki, Suze Orman, or Dave Ramsey. I didn't go to school to study finance or economics, and I don't have an MBA. I'm a woman who spent recklessly and got into a lot of debt, and I went through a ton of pain as a result of it. It turns out that the answer for me was a Spending Fast. By making that one big decision to start the Spending Fast, I in effect also made a ton of little decisions. Even though that decision required sacrifice and hard work, it also made my life a whole lot easier. The Spending Fast enabled me to get out of debt very, very quickly, after years of feeling like it would be completely impossible. This book is about how I did it, but it's also about what I learned along the way. The changes I made, the realizations I had, and how I turned these realizations into a brand-new, healthy relationship with money.

At the end of each chapter you'll find a list of things you can do as you're reading along to help you throughout the process. These "Let's Do This!" lists show you the actions I took at each stage of the Spending Fast. They're bite-sized steps that you can take to become debt-free just like I did with the Spending Fast.

I Don't Care How Much You Owe or How Much You Make

It doesn't matter what kind of debt you have. Maybe you've never used a credit card in your life (and I bow to you), but you're struggling to pay your student loans. My debt was a wicked combination of credit card debt and educational loans. Some people are stuck paying off giant medical bills. Or maybe you just convinced yourself that you deserve European vacations every year even though they're completely out of the range of your budget. Maybe you lost your job and didn't have a cushion to fall back on, so you fell on your credit cards instead, maxing them out in the process. Maybe your debt seemed relatively small compared to that of your friends, so you never addressed it, but you want to now. Maybe your senior years caught up with you, and you haven't put any money aside. My point is, it doesn't matter if you made some bad decisions (who hasn't?) or if you're saddled with massive student loans. The process I followed works no matter what situation you're in. You can use the Spending Fast method to get out of debt quickly—or to save money ASAP.

It also doesn't matter how much money you make. Being in debt is not the natural result of making a small salary. Countless people who earn large salaries have also gotten themselves deeply in debt by overspending or losing their income. My point is that getting out of debt is about facing the choices you've made and it's about having the guts to turn your situation around. Being debt-free didn't *happen* to me. It wasn't luck that got me out of debt. It wasn't chance. I'm debt-free because I made the choice to be, and you can too. Also, I want you to know that you don't have to do it alone. At the time of this writing, readers of AndThenWeSaved.com have saved over a million dollars using the Spending Fast and Spending Diet methods—and the number keeps going up! My website has many helpful tools and strategies to support you, and you can connect with other Spending Fasters on the And Then We Saved social media pages—Facebook (facebook.com/AndThenWeSaved), Pinterest, Instagram, Snapchat, and Twitter (@annanewelljones).

Please don't give up before you even get started by telling yourself it's just not going to happen on your yearly salary of $20,000, $30,000, or $150,000. Your journey toward being debt-free is not about the number on your paycheck; it's about your commitment to developing a new, healthier relationship with money. You *absolutely* can do this! Don't let *debt,* of all things, keep you from living the life you were meant to live.

CHAPTER 1

And I Kept Buying Even After the Money Was Gone

December 29 . . .

Decked out in layers of sweaters and wearing a pair of long johns under my jeans, I sat anxiously on a crowded and sniffly flight to visit my Midwestern family for Christmas. I was alone and wedged in a middle seat between two strangers when I hit my financial bottom. That December marked 8.8 years of my being in debt, and it signaled the thirtieth month in a row that I had rolled money from my overdraft account to my checking account to cover my excessive overspending.

At that moment on the plane, I owed exactly $23,605.10.

Now, I know that $23,605.10 is not as much as some people's debt, but the point is: it was bad enough for me. There was a heaviness associated with my debt, and it suffocated me even when I was not consciously thinking about it. Some days, I could completely ignore the way my debts pulled me and angled my decisions, and other days I neatly justified them by reminding myself that a hearty part of the total amount was just old college loans, which our society deems a "good" debt (according to *Forbes,* the outstanding national student debt balance as of February 2014 totaled $1.08 trillion). The other part of my debt was made up of a combination of consumer debt, approximately $6,000 (slightly lower than the average credit card balance of $7,327), and a loan (which I'd enthusiastically vowed to pay back) my parents took out on my behalf for my college education.

It was on that crowded plane that my financial life finally became real. What was it about *that* flight, *that* day, and *that* moment that caused my in-air epiphany? I don't even really know the answer. Maybe it was the pause in the day that I was allowed to take on that brief flight. Maybe it was because it was the first time in a while that I had been alone to think, to be in my own head. It could have been how surrounded I felt by my fellow seatmates. How they wrapped me up in their presence, how I was hemmed in on all sides, and how there was no way out. No way out of my debt, no way out of the plane.

During that flight I was able to fully grasp the scope of how unmanageable my life had become. I was able to see that I no longer had any control.

On the outside I'm sure I looked calm. I was still sitting there nicely minding my own business, listening to music, eating the greasy peanuts and drinking the guilty pleasure pop. I was still squeezed between the strangers and hating the middle seat, and I was still regretting my choice to wear the long johns under my jeans. But inside, I was changing; I was becoming willing to take action, to make tough and uncomfortable decisions. At that moment I was ready, motivated, and energized. I committed to myself: *I will finally be done with my debt!* This thought was quickly followed by *Well . . . at least the credit card debt—that at least seems* kinda *doable!*

I believe now that I had to make the mistakes I made to get to that point on that flight. I had to hit my financial bottom, and I don't think I would have been able to do what I needed to do to eliminate my debt had I not reached that level of demoralization and desperation. While I'm thankful for that now, I wasn't as grateful for it at the time. I didn't realize how often I would think back to that moment on the plane and remember those feelings of being completely swallowed up by the unmanageability of my debt.

It was those gut feelings—the *Oh my gosh, this has* got *to end*—that propelled me to keep going with the Spending Fast when I really wanted to quit.

Married to the Thrill of Spending

But I'm getting ahead of myself. First, I need to tell you how I wound up in all of this debt in the first place. That December marked the seventh month of my brand-new marriage. My wedding to Aaron was simple by most standards. We'd met a couple years before, when he saw my photography online. Aaron sent me a message on MySpace (now that MySpace is "vintage social media," it's less embarrassing to admit how we met than it used to be) saying that he liked my photography. I thought, *Hmm, that's nice, and he's kind of cute.* Later, he messaged me to ask, "Have you been on any photo excursions recently?" Since I'd never heard anyone actually use the word *excursion* in real life (I had only seen it in books), I was intrigued.

I'd just gotten out of a six-and-a-half-year relationship and was ready to have some fun. My life had recently changed in a lot of ways, and even though I didn't really know Aaron yet, I figured anyone who used the word "excursion" probably couldn't harm me. Just to be careful, though, I called a friend before he was scheduled to arrive on our first date to tell her all the details about him and the date, just in case I went missing.

Turns out my gut was right and he wasn't a grizzly disguised as a bunny. He was totally harmless. Aaron was (is) a good, solid man, who could grow a thick beard, but more importantly, he actually followed through on things. We talked about going camping, and we actually went camping. I can't tell you how impressed I was by that. A guy with follow-through?! Who knew that was possible? Three years later, we were married on a windy May day in a one-room schoolhouse in a "botanical garden" that wasn't very botanical at all, but we went with it anyway. A reception at an art gallery followed, and the whole event was approximately 90 percent over budget. Being over budget wasn't anything new to me, because at that point it was my way of life.

My parents had given us $3,000, a small chunk of money relative to the cost of weddings, and I liked being able to buy what I needed and, more importantly, what I just plain wanted for the wedding. For instance, throughout the course of planning our wedding I ended up buying six different headpieces. I was in a "choice overload vortex" (it's a real thing). I couldn't make a decision on just one, and heck no, I wasn't going to make the wrong choice, so I decided to just purchase each piece I was considering. I ended up with a thick satin fabric headband, a thin ivory headband, a huge pink fabric flower, a papier-mâché flower and twigs "crown," a fluffy 1920s-esque feather clip, and a midlength, slightly fluffy, but not too fluffy, ivory tulle veil, which proved to be the ultimate winner.

Not being able to decide just meant that I erred on the side of buying *more.* And when Aaron didn't want to spend the money on things for the wedding, like eight samples of invitations or 275 mini candles, I decided that I would just pay for them myself. That year my tax refund and credit cards paid for the balance between what my parents contributed and what I wanted. I kept Aaron carefully sheltered from the reality of my secret spending habits. I figured that if he didn't know how much I was spending, then he wouldn't be allowed to protest on the grounds of cost, and I could craft the wedding I wanted.

According to *CNNMoney*, the average wedding in the United States in 2014 cost $30,000, and there was no way we were going to hit that amount, so I felt really good about things. At one point I even thought, *Look at how conservative I'm being! Dang! I'm basically a cheapskate!* But guess what didn't stop when the planning did?

My spending.

Planning my wedding proved to be just the vehicle I needed to morph my kind-of-bad spending habits into really bad ones, and my overspending only continued and got stronger after Aaron and I had our walk down the aisle.

Spending Gone Rogue

My natural inclination is to spend money. I have never been a person who is *excited* to set money aside. (Never. Not even now.) Saving money sounded completely boring and stupid, and savings accounts sounded great—for other people. Oh, sure, at times I would try; I would put money into a savings account for a couple weeks, but actually leaving it in there? Uh-uh. Not a chance.

Routinely, I spent money before it even truly existed in my life. One year an over-priced tax preparer told me, "You'll be getting a $525 refund." As soon as those words fell out of her mouth, that money (plus some) was already spent. Minutes after leaving the dimly lit, pale-green-carpeted corporate office, I was busy filling my cart at the closest store I could find. I packed it with pale blue pillowcases, the newest mascara that Drew Barrymore, Ellen DeGeneres, and Queen Latifah insisted would be amazing (hey, I want to be amazing), a silver lamp base and coordinating off-white linen lamp shade that I thought looked classy (it did), laundry detergent scented like a moonlit breeze, two sports bras, work pants, work shoes, a colander, a pizza cutter (because I always really wanted one), hair dye, a toaster, rosy (but not too rosy) blush, eyeliner, cereal, a glass cake stand with a dome top, and a whole bunch of stuff I can't even remember. I considered everything I put in my cart to be something I *needed,* so naturally, buying these things was okay.

And so it came to be that the months preceding my in-air financial meltdown were filled with the accumulation of even more debt.

It didn't help that it was December, which is synonymous with spending. Lots of spending. And overspending. In fact, according to the National Retail Federation, spending increased 4 percent to a whopping $616.1 billion in the last two months of 2014—the highest level since 2011. I wanted my family to know that I loved them, and at the time that meant buying them things. In my mind, material items equaled love. So, throughout the eleven months leading up to the holidays, I would secretly jot down things that family and friends mentioned liking. Little light-yellow sticky notes overflowed with gift ideas. I wanted to believe that when I bought my sister a moss terrarium it showed her I cared. When my mom said, "You're so thoughtful, Anna," I didn't want her to ever change her mind. I also wanted my family and friends to think that I was okay financially and not broke and overwhelmed, as I really was. I didn't want them to know that I couldn't keep up anymore, or that I would never be able to catch up. I liked looking like a success, and I liked having the newest and best things. Looking back, I see that my pride was partially responsible for keeping me in debt. Buying made the good days better; it helped ease the strain of the bad days; it gave me something to do when I was bored or needed to destress. Spending gave me something to look forward to, think about, and plan on.

And I kept buying even when the money was gone or close to being gone. I knew that my overdraft account or my credit card always had my back. Several nights a month, I clicked the necessary boxes to transfer money electronically from my credit card to my checking account as a way to manage my unruly spending habits and allow myself to continue my financial decline and state of denial. I clicked the buttons as fast as I could and quickly closed the Web browser with the little "x" to keep myself from really having to see the mess I was creating.

The fees that stacked up as a result of my cutting it close too often were mixed into the big pile of debt that was already there, and in relation to how much money I already owed, those fees hardly seemed like anything to worry about. On rare occasions I would get motivated to change my ways, and that would result in a small jolt of progress toward getting some of my debt paid off. But then I would get discouraged by the *painfully* slow debt repayment process and overspend yet again. I had tried things like budgeting, getting a part-time job specifically to pay back the debt, and good old-fashioned cutting back (described in chapter 2), and it just didn't work for me. Nothing stuck. I had resigned to dying with my debt.

Setting Myself Up for a Miracle

When I decided to stop my spending, I didn't have many of the details sorted out and didn't know how it would really work. All I knew was that it sounded extremely terrible and super-thrilling all at once. But while I was on the plane I did manage to figure out a couple of things. First, I would stop spending money. I'd call it a Spending Fast and I would spend money only on absolute necessities. Next, I would start a blog to keep myself accountable. And I would do it for a year. At that moment, I didn't know how much my life was about to change, and I had no clue that I was setting myself up for a miracle.

Going Back Before Going Forward

A few days before the Spending Fast was scheduled to begin I made a few last-minute purchases. My plan was to try to think about everything I could possibly need in the upcoming year. This is what I bought: two cans of aerosol dry shampoo from a TV infomercial, elastic ribbon hair ties, a linen screen-printed calendar complete with happy-looking seahorses floating about, and a set of three patterned rubber stamps. I had no defense against the dry shampoo. That guy had hypnotic powers, and that was that. My coworker had some of the hair ties and I thought they were cute, so I had to have some too. I figured the stamp set was a really great idea so I could make cards for people throughout the year, and that way I wouldn't be a complete deadbeat friend and family member. At least then I could write in the card, "You're not getting anything except for this card I made. You're the best! Happy birthday!"

My last-minute preparatory purchases turned out to be completely useless in my getting-out-of-debt quest—except to further prove why I needed the Spending Fast so badly. There was no reason I bought the way I did; an object just needed to catch my attention. I was like a cat that got transfixed by a laser beam or a sunny spot on the floor. I was an easy sell.

Beginning the Fast

At the beginning of the Spending Fast, my feelings about my financial defeat were still really fresh, so it was easy to stay focused on why I was doing what I was. My goal was to attempt to make a dent in my credit card debt. It was easy to be really gung ho about it in the beginning. After the first couple of weeks, though, it got harder. Looking back, I can now see that the period from week two up to the three-month mark was by far the hardest part of the Spending Fast.

As I was starting out, I told every single person I knew that I was going to start a Spending Fast. I explained that this meant I would no longer be going out to eat with them, to movies, or on trips. Some resisted and said I didn't need to be "so extreme." But I knew what needed to be done, and if that meant no dinners out for the year, that was a reality I was okay with.

I wrote out all my debts and their interest rates. I went through the previous three months of my bank statements to get a very clear idea of where my money was going. And then, armed with the reality of my spending ways, I created my Wants and Needs List (I'll show you how to do this in chapter 5). This list turned out to be intense. I was getting ready to cut out all unnecessary, superfluous spending and spend only on what I absolutely needed to survive.

Thinking About Life in a New Way

Throughout the year of the Spending Fast, I figured out how to deal with all sorts of social situations, how to get really creative with my wardrobe, how to spend less on groceries, how to simply explain what the Spending Fast is, how to fill all the extra time, how to be more present, how to avoid temptation, how to deal with not doing the Spending Fast perfectly, and how to ask for help. But really, through it all, what it came down to is: The Spending Fast taught me how to live in a simpler, more intentional way.

My life was no longer consumed by material objects.

At the end of every month I reviewed the grand total that I was able to send to the creditors. I started to compete with myself—each month I wanted to see if I could beat the previous month's numbers. After the first month I had $505 left after paying my bills, money that in the past I would have spent on random purchases. The second month, over $900! Throughout the course of the year, saving ended up becoming as fun as spending, and I was more shocked than anyone that the Spending Fast was actually working. After one year of the Spending Fast I paid off $18,175.45 in debt! And since I still had some debt left, I started a Spending Diet (more on that later). After working through my Debt Hit List (described in chapter 6) at the end of the fifteenth month, I was able to send the very last payment to my creditors!

I was finally, *finally* out of debt!

That $23,605.10 in debt that I was convinced I would die with? *GONE.*

Even better? I was able to make it happen on my $33,000 salary as a clerk for the state, and my husband's income didn't contribute to my debt payoff total. Not a penny. If anyone out there is thinking my husband was footing the bill for me while

I did the Fast, he'll be the first one to tell you he didn't. I get into the details of how a Spending Fast works for couples later on. But I'll also be totally honest: I'm really fortunate because my kind parents did choose to match some of my student loan payments (the matched payments ended up being approximately 9 percent of the total paid off through the Spending Fast). I know I'm lucky that they did this, because every single cent helps.

> *I've spent the last year reading about how to simplify my life and spend less. I even moved to an apartment that was closer to work so I could save money by riding my bike. It always seemed like something came up—bake sales, luncheons, drinks with friends, and so on. I never took that final step of saying no and not buying things. AndThenWeSaved.com has finally shown me that saying no has been someone else's problem too. I'm so encouraged.*
>
> *—Molly*

Living with Less to Achieve a More Authentic Life

Being debt-free means that I'm now able to live on a lot less money. A couple years after I got out of debt, I was able to go part-time with my day job so I could focus more on what I really love doing, photography. And when our son was born we were able to entertain the idea of one of us working from home instead of sending him to day care full-time. My life looks a lot more like what I want it to, and it's all because I'm not weighed down by a huge obligation to pay off debt. Now my family is able to make decisions that reflect who we truly are *today*, and we can work on shaping what we want our lives to look like in the future. Being debt-free has given us a new kind of life and a new kind of freedom.

How This Book Will Help

If you want to have what I have—a debt-free and autonomous life—this book will show you how to do it. Here is an overview of the Spending Fast method, which I'll go through chapter by chapter in the rest of the book.

Define Your Ideal Life

The first step in the Spending Fast plan is to determine your priorities by putting pen to paper to define what your ideal life looks like. You must define it to get it. I want you to think less about the exterior specifications and focus more on the feelings you want to experience every day. Once you've identified those feelings, we're going to work toward getting you to see that achieving them has little to do with spending money and everything to do with taking action.

Decide to Be Done with Debt Once and for All

The Spending Fast technique requires a lot of commitment and dedication. It's a way to get dramatic results in a relatively short amount of time, but you have to be ready to go forward with all you've got. You have to be all in. If you've tried many other methods that just didn't work, chances are you're ready for the Spending Fast.

THE *I WOULD, BUTS*: COMMON EXCUSES FOR NOT DOING A SPENDING FAST

"I don't make enough money."
"I'm already paying as much on my debt as I can."
"I have kids."
"My partner doesn't want to do it with me."
"I don't have that kind of willpower."
"It's too hard."
"It's too drastic."
"I have *a lot* more debt than you did."
"I have vacations and events coming up that I have to spend money on."
"Life will suck on the Spending Fast."
"I'm dating and it will be awkward."

"I'm planning a wedding."

"The holidays are coming."

"My friends won't like it if I have to turn down their invites."

Set a Time Frame for Your Spending Fast

We'll discuss how to choose a time length that's right for you and your Spending Fast. I recommend a year, so you can get past the difficult beginning part (when all your habits are getting changed) and into the real benefits part (when your debt is being paid off). A year can seem long day to day, but at the end you'll be surprised how quickly it goes by. However, whether you choose to do a Spending Fast for a weekend, a week, a couple of months, or a year, you'll still get results that will positively affect your financial situation. While I've got your back no matter what you decide, and I've told you I think a year is the way to go, know there are benefits to mini-Fasts as well. Obviously a weekend-long Spending Fast isn't likely to eliminate most debts, but you can learn a few things about yourself. Tracking spending over a weekend will still highlight some of those deadly autopilot spending habits (you spent how much on cold-pressed juice?). You'll see how much cash you drop socializing with friends, and how much you can save by eating those lentils you had in the cupboard rather than picking up a take-out burrito. If a mini-Fast motivates you and helps you reanalyze how you approach spending in different areas in your life, then it's worth doing.

Make It Known

I'll talk you through telling your friends and family about your decision to do a Spending Fast, and you'll be introduced to the Get Out of Debt Pledge. You'll also get to read some testimonials from others who are committed to getting out of debt. It's super-inspiring to read the pledges on AndThenWeSaved.com. I always read them when I need a burst of motivation.

Find People Like You

You'll be most successful with your Spending Fast if you can find your tribe. I'll go over ways to find people who share your goal. One resource is the And Then We Saved Facebook page. There people share their questions, struggles, accomplishments, setbacks, tips, tricks, and, most importantly, their getting-out-of-debt successes. In a society where five-bedroom houses and huge seven-seat SUVs are the norm, it's vital that we get reminders that we aren't alone in our dreams to live debt-free.

Create the Plan

I'll explain how to make a Debt Hit List. This will determine the order in which you will eliminate each debt.

Lower Your Interest Rates

Sometimes you can get companies to lower your interest rate by making a two-minute call. I'll provide you with a slew of tips and techniques for a successful negotiation.

Create the Backbone for Your Fast

The Wants and Needs List is the backbone of the Spending Fast. A quick overview: On the Needs side of your list, you'll include the necessities you need to live, and on the Wants side, you'll put everything that is an "extra" in your life. Your Wants and Needs List can (and will) be different from mine because it's generated based on the priorities in *your* life, which will differ from the priorities in *my* life.

Spending Only on Needs

This is the simple-but-not-easy part of the Spending Fast, and we'll talk about the best ways to manage Needs-only spending.

Change Your Thinking

We'll be going over what to do if you find yourself starting to feel bummed out during your Spending Fast. I'll tell you how to shift your perspective and keep having fun (just the free kind).

Stay Committed and Continue

It's unrealistic to think that mistakes won't happen. I'll go over how to refocus and get back to the plan.

Attack the Debt!

I'll show you how to figure out how much to send to each creditor, how to get competitive with yourself, and how to track your savings month to month. This is where you'll start to see all your hard work pay off. As the amount of money you save grows each month, and your debt starts to go down, you'll be more inspired than ever to do what it takes to live debt-free.

CHAPTER 2

From Spender to Saver

Wanting to be debt-free is easy. I mean, who doesn't want that? I can't think of anyone who doesn't want to have the weight of debt lifted from their lives. But actually getting to the point of deciding *Yes! I'll do whatever it takes to become debt-free* is a completely different story. For this reason, even though I hated my debt, it was a long time before I was able to make any lasting changes to my financial life. In fact, I tried just about every traditional method for getting out of debt that I could think of. The following are techniques I tried:

Regular old "cutting back": I would be motivated for a day or two and then I'd quickly lose steam when I decided that my debt probably wasn't that bad after all. I justified it by saying, "Everyone's got debt!"

Budgeting: I tried budgeting and failed miserably at it. For one, I found that budgeting allowed too much of a gray area for discretionary spending. Plus, I could never decide if things like eating out counted for the Entertainment category or the Food/Groceries category. I feel silly admitting that not knowing what category to put things in was a reason budgeting didn't work for me, but it's the truth. For me, budgeting was too tedious.

Getting a job specifically to pay off my credit card debt: I applied for a job at a popular retail chain, Gap. I was hoping to work evenings following my forty-hour-a-week job with the state, but even during the interview I was torn. Part of me was thinking, *I'll be able to pay off my credit cards!* while another part was thinking, *I'm going to have the best wardrobe! Oh! Look at that shirt!* When I didn't get the job, I felt conflicted: happy that I wouldn't be adding twenty additional hours to my workweek but also disappointed that I wouldn't be able to even try to make a dent in those credit card bills. That is, if I could figure out a way to control my spending—which even I knew was a long shot.

I know now that had I been set loose in that clothing store and constantly tempted by the newest designs, I most likely would not have been successful at using the money from that job to chip away at my debt anyway. At that point I wasn't desperate enough to be done with my debt. I had no tools in place, no history of success to rely on to help me change my ways, and I hadn't yet learned how to tell myself no. So getting that job would have been a very bad idea indeed.

Living with Debt to Fit In

I had no idea that all that stuff I was pining for wasn't really what I wanted. What I wanted was a better, different way of living, and I was going about it all wrong. I was trying to change the way my life looked on the outside with the hopes that it would change how I felt on the inside—and it didn't work.

I thought of myself as a smart person, someone who wasn't swayed by clever marketing slogans or trendy styles. But what I thought about myself was actually totally wrong. I wanted to think I didn't care if everyone was wearing a certain type of pants or a certain color of shirt that season, but this simply wasn't true. Even if I couldn't admit it to myself, I wanted to fit in more than anything else, and material items gave me a way to attempt to make that happen.

You see, as a kid, I was painfully shy. Often I would go days without speaking a word to people outside my family. In middle school I realized that even if I was labeled The Shy Kid or That Quiet Girl, I could feel a little cool and "right" if I had the same kinds of clothes as the popular kids. If they had Hypercolor T-shirts and CK One perfume, then that's what I wanted. A Starter jacket and scrunchies in every color? Yes. I needed those too.

I thought I could use material objects to show the kids in my school that I fit in, even if my anxiety wouldn't let me talk to them. However, it didn't work and I didn't fool anyone. But, even as I became an adult, the idea of using material things to fit in had stuck with me. It seems just about everyone wants to fit in, especially when our place in the social hierarchy or our status feels threatened. In fact, studies show that we're more likely to buy expensive luxury goods or even consume higher-calorie foods when we feel like we're "lower" or "less than" others.

The Spending Fast helped me break the cycle. It taught me that I was capable of saying no to myself. And that helped to build up my self-esteem and self-worth. I realized I didn't need the latest fashions to feel good about who I was. I didn't even notice this was happening until I realized how proud I felt with each check I sent to the bill collectors. By telling myself no I was, in effect, slowly empowering myself. I was saying, *I don't need this item to prove I have value,* and *Life goes on just fine even if I don't have the same new things as my coworker.*

Every time I stuck to my getting-out-of-debt mission, I was taking my life back. I was feeling more and more like the me I knew I was deep inside, the one that was okay with myself with no makeup, zits, and unruly hair. The external objects in my life were losing their importance, and other priorities were taking their place. I was happy to think about living a life where I didn't have to be perfect to be okay.

The Negative Impacts of Debt

My debt wasn't just a giant bill that I constantly worried I'd never pay off. While I didn't know it at the time, my debt impacted my life in many negative ways beyond financially. I was seriously limiting my choices by being so heavily in debt. I was glad to learn from my amazing readers on AndThenWeSaved.com that I wasn't alone in experiencing major negativity in my life because of the debt I carried. For me, being in debt meant a loss of freedom. For others, it meant everything from having limited career choices to feeling like life was not able to move forward.

"Being debt-free would mean having the freedom to know I could pursue whatever career I wanted, not just the one that paid the most."
"I feel like my debt is holding me back, and I can't do the things I want."
"Being debt-free would be like starting from scratch."

It doesn't matter how much debt you have, or how you got it. Whether you're in debt because you went to medical school or bought stupid stuff you couldn't afford, debt is emotionally crippling. When you're anxious about money and have to take your debt into account when making choices, you're simply not living your best life. The more I thought about this, the more inspired and determined I became to get rid of the restrictions my debt was placing on my life.

My Dream of an Autonomous Life

When I was thinking about doing the Spending Fast, one of the things that appealed to me was becoming autonomous. Autonomy is about being self-governing: being able to make decisions based on your own (and your family's own) best interests. I had no idea what autonomy would feel like. I could only imagine that It. Would. Be. Amazing. And so I found myself daydreaming about how great it would be to not owe money to student loan lenders; banks; credit card, mortgage, and insurance companies; and, most of all, to my parents.

See, right out of high school I went to this extremely expensive photography school. My parents didn't want me to go to this college because of the cost, but I was wielding a dream, and had lots of optimism and absolutely no concept of money. I quickly assured them that if they would take out the parent portion of the loans, I would be able to pay them back "in no time."

Looking back, although I'm glad I went to photography school, I simply shouldn't have insisted on going to such an expensive one. If I had done more research, I'd have found there were cheaper options available that would have resulted in my taking on much less debt. But I was young and dreamed of someday become a *National Geographic* photographer, which only fueled my willingness to sign on the dotted line toward heaps of debt.

Years later my dream changed into one far less intoxicating: More than anything I wanted to be free from the hopeless cycle of debt and overspending madness I'd become so accustomed to. What I really wanted was to be autonomous, self-governing. I needed to get current with my debts and get my financial life in order so I could make day-to-day choices that really reflected who I was *today,* not who I was *yesterday.* I needed to clear up the past. Remembering this goal kept me motivated as I started down the road of the Spending Fast.

Becoming my true self was my dream. Now it's time to figure out yours.

What Does Your Ideal Life Look Like?

I wanted to be able to live autonomously. I knew that each day I wanted to feel truly content with myself and my actions, and I just wanted to be happy and content in general. Maybe you don't know right off the top of your head what you're trying to accomplish, the way I did. If that's the case, rather than thinking about what superficial types of things you might possess (such as a new car, house, or wardrobe), I want you to think about what your ideal life feels like. By thinking about how your ideal life *feels* rather than how it looks, you'll be able to work toward achieving those inner feelings even if what your life looks like on the outside remains exactly the same.

Happiness and contentment are definitely not unique things to want in one's life. You might want the same things, or maybe you want to feel more alive and present or more confident and strong. What's the feeling you want most? Take a minute to think about the times that you've felt the most alive. Try to recall those visceral, gut-level "this is what life is all about!" moments.

Write down those memories that stand out and their corresponding feelings. These feelings are the ones we're after. You'll come to realize that tapping into those moments where you felt most alive has nothing to do with what is going on externally. And they definitely have nothing to do with the material objects you're surrounded by.

Here's how I do it. When I think of happiness, in my mind I hear laughter. So I seek out chances to laugh. I try not to take myself too seriously, and I really appreciate people who have a good sense of humor. A few years ago I was given a small bright-yellow blank book. I keep it by my bed and, every chance I get, I fill it with notes about what makes me laugh. I have everything in there from funny expressions I hear throughout the day to observations that crack me up. The great thing about keeping this little book is that what I write down doesn't have to make sense or be funny to anyone but me.

I try to remember the times when I feel content. Usually I feel content after a good workout, after I clear out my e-mail inbox, or after I check off a whole lot of things on my to-do list. For me, contentment comes after I *do something,* which means I have to take *action.* When I was deep in debt I could never find contentment because I was always searching for something more, something I could never find.

Don't Confuse a Shopping High with True Happiness

Earlier, I said that the positive feelings we all seek in life can't be bought. Now, you may be thinking that this isn't true, because you may be one of those people who have feelings of elation when you get a great deal when you're shopping. If this is you, then I want you to focus on how fleeting those feelings are. Was it the item you bought that made you happy or were you seeking the high of getting a good deal? Did a wave of guilt come over you for spending the money? And have you often found that you regret purchases once the shopping high has waned?

It's important to note the difference between what you associate with being the source of your elation and what actually causes the rush. It's easy to connect those heightened feelings of hunting and capturing with the acquisition of material goods, but honestly you could get those same feelings without spending a dime. Here's an example. When I was younger, I played a lot of sports, and in many ways, buying a great item has similarities to nailing a goal. I would stalk the ball, overcome my competition, and come out victorious when I scored. That was an unbeatable feeling, and it's one that parallels spotting a great item, getting to it before anyone else, and bringing it home. The difference is, of course, that scoring a goal doesn't cost money and doesn't put you into debt.

The Things That Make Us Happiest Aren't for Sale

Once you have a clear idea of the times that you've felt truly alive, you'll be able to see that it's those feelings you're after, not the new shirt or boots that you once thought led you to happiness. You'll be able to achieve these positive emotions without spending a lot, and without accumulating more and more stuff in an effort to experience those feelings. You'll feel much better about embarking on the Spending Fast when you realize that you don't need your attachment to spending nearly as much as you thought you did.

Finding other ways to mimic that shopper's high will undoubtedly help you in your Spending Fast, because you'll be able to replace the spending with another activity. This step is very important in the getting-out-of-debt process.

Is the Spending Fast Right for You?

The Spending Fast method is a drastic approach to getting out of debt, and it might not be a good fit for everyone. If you're living off credit cards for your daily needs and just to get by, do the Spending Fast—but not with the intention of becoming debt-free. Instead, do the Spending Fast with the goal of gaining some stable footing. Which in this case means not relying on credit cards for your daily expenses. If you are not using your credit cards to feed yourself each day, I still recommend that you hold off on trying the Spending Fast method until you've explored other methods first. I say this because a Spending Fast requires a lot of sacrifice, dedication, and commitment. When I did the Spending Fast, I had hit rock bottom, and I was desperate enough to make the needed sacrifices. Giving up eating out and going to movies (among other things) seemed like the least I could do to have a new life, and it turns out those things quickly lost the appeal they once had as soon as I was committed to my plan.

If you too have felt as if you'll die with your debt, if you struggle with a deep urge to spend every cent in your account, and if you've tried a range of other getting-out-of-debt methods, then the Spending Fast might be the answer to your prayers.

Living More Honestly by Breaking Spending Habits

Often we get so wrapped up in the habits of spending that we don't ever really evaluate how or why we spend the way we do. We've just always done it a certain way, so we continue on. But once you start spending less, chances are that a more authentic life will reveal itself to you—one that's full of the emotions that make you feel really alive and content; one that isn't stuffed to the brim with junk and clutter that needs to be managed and maintained. New, stronger relationships will be built and old relationships will have new life infused into them. Later on in the book, we'll talk more about these relationships—and how to break the news to your friends and family to get them excited about (or at least accepting of) your new way of life.

I DIDN'T PUT MONEY IN SAVINGS (DURING THE SPENDING FAST)— HERE'S WHY

Yes. You read that right. I didn't put money aside in a savings account while I was doing the Spending Fast. I didn't even *consider* saving one cent until I was 100 percent debt-free. When I tried to save in the past I would put money into my savings, and then slowly but surely it would dwindle. Before I knew it, that chunk of money had somehow fizzled away, and I was left with nothing to show for it. Saving money is a good thing to do—I *get* that. When I started the Spending Fast I made a choice to get out of debt as soon as I possibly could. I wanted to put every extra penny that I didn't spend on necessities right toward my debt, so that it would be gone ASAP. Many professional financial planners advocate paying down your debt *and* saving at the same time. While I'm not saying that's a bad thing to do, I knew it was not the right approach *for me*. What worked in my life was: get outta debt hella fast, and *then* switch my focus to saving *big*.

It was the process of undergoing the Spending Fast that changed my relationship with money permanently. The Fast taught me that I could say no, make better choices, and not spend like a madwoman. Until I figured that out, any money I might have saved would have ended up paying for emergencies that weren't really emergencies at all. I think it's great if you can say, "Hey, I'd like to have a $1,000 cushion in my budget, so I'm going to basically start billing myself $100 each month until I have that amount in savings." I knew I wasn't capable of doing that successfully, so the Spending Fast also served as a sort of financial cleanse. I emerged from it with a clearer idea about how to deal with money, as well as the maturity to realize that saving was the next step in my journey to being financially responsible. So for now the decision to sock money away in savings is completely up to you. I'll talk about saving money in more detail later in the book when I get into the details of the Spending Diet.

$ Let's Do This!

- ❑ Write down everything you've already done to try to get out of debt.
- ❑ Write down how your debt has negatively impacted your life. How has debt held you back? How has it affected your relationships and decisions?
- ❑ Ask yourself: *What would my life look like if money wasn't an issue?* What would you be doing differently? How would you feel?
- ❑ How will you feel *when* you are finally out of debt?
- ❑ Decide for yourself if you're ready to get out of debt and if you're willing to go to the lengths needed to get there.

CHAPTER 3

Getting Started: "Today Is the Day I Decide to Become Debt-Free"

You already know that I was committed to the Spending Fast for an entire year, but you need to decide what works best for you. It's tempting to overanalyze everything before you commit. Is a year too long? Will a year of not buying new music/books/kitchen utensils result in a loss of sanity? Am I being a wimp if I do just a month? The bottom line is you need to decide on the right time frame and then get started.

Setting a Time Frame for Your Spending Fast

As you begin your Spending Fast, you may find that your friends and family have a lot of questions for you about how you'll handle different situations, but the truth is that you don't need to have an answer to every question. All you need to do is to make the decision to *begin*. Once you decide on a start date and pick a time frame, your glorious end date will be set. Spending Fasts can be done over a weekend, a month, six months, a year, or for years. You'll reap some benefits no matter the length of time you choose, but I do highly recommend following it for a year, as I did.

Why a Year Is the Ideal Amount of Time for a Spending Fast

By committing to a yearlong Spending Fast, you'll be able to get past the beginning part of the process, which is incredibly hard. That's when your lifestyle gets its major initial overhaul, but once that stage is over, you can get into a groove and start experiencing the real benefits of the Spending Fast.

You'll tell your friends and family members you're doing this crazy financial experiment, and then after the first couple of months they'll realize that you weren't joking and that your Spending Fast really is going to happen for an entire year.

A year gives you enough time to start to change your habits. Instead of your old automatic response of "Yes, let's go to lunch!" when invited out by a friend, you'll reply, "Yes, let's get together at lunchtime and eat our lunches in the park!"

It gets easier to tell yourself no. Seriously, this was a big one for me. I had no idea that I was basically a super-big two-year-old having tantrums inside my head every time I even considered telling myself I couldn't spend money whenever I wanted to. By the time I ended the Spending Fast, I was less of a spoiled brat and had grown to at least age fourteen or so.

As time goes on, you will save more money. Sure, you can do a weekend-long Spending Fast and save maybe $50 (which is great! Hey, I'm not raining on any parades! Saving is saving!), but the longer you do the Spending Fast, the more debt you'll eliminate, and you just might get some money into your savings account too.

Your habits start to get cemented and your thinking changes as you work through the Spending Fast. There's no way to do a Spending Fast for a year and not have your habits permanently change. After my yearlong Spending Fast I couldn't look at clothing shops the same way, and I'm so thankful for that. The fewer belongings I had, the more grateful I became for the things I did have. At one point during my Spending Fast, my husband gave me half a pound of nice ground coffee as a gift and I savored every single sip of coffee I made from it. Before, having special coffee would've been something I took for granted. Coffee? Yeah, I drink it every day. No big deal—but not after the Spending Fast. Doing the Spending Fast made me extremely thankful for any little luxury that came into my life.

Not spending money becomes fun. I know you think I'm making this one up—who would've guessed that a major Spender would be having fun while implementing a ban on spending? But it's true, it happened. The longer I did the Spending Fast, the more I wanted to save and find new ways to save. I wanted to cut out any extra spending, and I wanted to send more money to the creditors. Each month as I wrote out the payments I liked to imagine that someone at the company was saying, "Heck, yeah! She's killing it!" Even though they probably didn't care and my payments were most likely processed by a computer, it was fun to imagine a person on the other side was cheering for me, too.

One thing to remember: When you do a yearlong Spending Fast, make sure to focus on your end date. Nothing is worse than starting something that seems very difficult and not seeing an end to it. A year can seem long day to day, but you'll be surprised how quickly it goes by. Trust me, you can do anything for a year.

Going Public with Your Spending Fast

Finding yourself in debt and not being able to easily get yourself out of it can feel very shameful and embarrassing. I did everything I could to keep people from seeing how broke I really was. With my cute tops, salon haircuts, $100 dinners out, and my yes reply to every invite and vacation, no one would've guessed that I was having a really hard time keeping my head above water.

Then I decided to make it public and said, "Hey, y'all, I've got a crapload of debt! This is me!" It felt scary and I felt vulnerable, but it was also very, very freeing. I no longer had to live the lie of pretending I had everything together. I could say, "Look at me being imperfect. I'm kind of a mess right now, but I'm willing to make some tough choices and changes. Come watch this train wreck unfold!"

I was so happy to be able to let my guard down and just be who I was. So I highly recommend that once you've set a time frame for your Spending Fast, you tell every single person you know that you're going to change your life by doing one. Put it on Facebook, put it on Instagram, put it on Twitter, YouTube, Pinterest, Snapchat, and Reddit. Tell people on the street, tell people at work, tell everyone everywhere. Telling people about your Spending Fast will not only liberate you to be yourself, it will also help you stay accountable. I figured that the more people I told, the better, because then I would be less likely to give up. And that's exactly what happened!

There was another benefit of telling everyone about my goal that I hadn't anticipated. When things felt awkward or got tricky socially, I was able to make the Spending Fast the scapegoat. I was able to say, "Oh! You know, I would *love* to go to the movie, but I've got this Spending Fast thing I'm doing!" If the person had already heard about what I was up to, they'd say, "That's right, I forgot," or "I don't think you told me about that. What's that all about?"

Research shows that by revealing your goals, you're in essence asking people for help in achieving them, and that by telling others about your goals, you create compelling motivation toward action.

Be prepared for the fact that everyone will have a lot of questions for you. That's okay! They're just curious. Remember not to get discouraged if you don't have an answer to every question they ask. You don't have to have all the answers. Also, you'll get different reactions from people. Some people will be thrilled for you (call me, I'll be thrilled for you—I promise!) and some people will be, uh, not so thrilled. Try to avoid letting the not-so-thrilled folks get you down. Some of my favorite responses came from my husband (he is now totally pro-Fast, by the way), who said, "Great. This is gonna suck," and my best friend, Shayla, who said, "Well, that doesn't sound very fun." You know the Spending Fast is the right decision for you, and that's all that matters. You don't have to justify your decision to anyone. Most people are just worried about how the Spending Fast will impact their relationship with you. Seriously, that is what's usually at the root of any guff they might give.

Why Going Public with Your Goals Works

If you were in any denial about your financial situation, your mind-set will change when you tell your friends and family honestly where you stand financially. No one wants to be humiliated, and if you don't stick to your goal, people will know when you have to fess up as they ask you how it's going. Since people will ask you about your Spending Fast all the time, it will keep your goal fresh in your mind, and you won't be able to get away from it even if you try.

Others knowing about your plan will motivate you to succeed. You'll want to tell everyone how great you're doing with your Spending Fast, because you'll be taking action in an area of your life that has been troubling you. Going public with your getting-out-of-debt goal will tell people exactly why you'll have to turn down some (if not most) invitations, which will help prevent your friends and family from taking your declining personally.

The Get Out of Debt Pledge

Once you've decided to start a Spending Fast, I recommend you take the Get Out of Debt Pledge. The pledge is your opportunity to lay it all on the line, where you'll write out your commitment to your deepest, truest, most inner self that you're ready to change your life and take the steps necessary to do what you must to finally become debt-free. By making the Get Out of Debt Pledge, you're freeing yourself from the cycle of guilt, remorse, and overspending. You're taking your life back by making the decision to live differently, to be free, and to be autonomous.

Here are some examples of pledges people have made (the names have been changed):

> *I'm in. I have debt totaling $12,000. I had just accepted that I would never get out of debt and was resigned to a life of making minimum payments and wasting the rest of my surplus money on entertainment and shopping. I feel hopeful.* —Frannie

> *All right. I'm doing it. I'm done with this tightening feeling I get in my chest when I think about how much money I owe. Nearly $73,000, mostly student loans, but there are a few credit cards in there as well. I'd like to have my debts paid off before I have kids, which I believe will give me more motivation and a sense of urgency. My Spending Fast starts today.* —Lauren

I have a huge amount of unsecured consumer debt that never gets smaller. I need the dramatic success of the Spending Fast to make me see that it is even possible. I've been in debt all my life, and I'm so tired of the fear and anxiety surrounding money. I have no idea of the positive forces this effort will unleash, but I'm looking forward to the journey.
—Sarah

I'm super-scared/excited, but I'm in! No unnecessary spending for me!
—Maddie

I am committing myself to a yearlong Spending Fast, starting right now! It is something I have known I needed to do for a long time, but I can't sweep it under the rug anymore. While it will be tough, I look at it as a challenge to rethink and refocus on what is truly important, and all the amazing things I can do instead of spending money, like spending more time with friends and family.
—Ashley

Count. Me. In. Currently going through a divorce and have about $16K in credit card debt. I have no retirement and no safety net. Woke up one morning this fall and realized that it's just me now. . . . Meaning, all those trips I've always wanted to take? I have to pay for them. All those great restaurants I want to eat at? I'm paying. There's no way I'm starting my new life in the red. . . . I'm gonna kick some financial ass.
—Jenny

My husband and I are in! We have modified our fast/diet with competition and incentives to make it more fun, and our friends and family are on board (and amused!). We hope—I mean plan—to knock out his $4K credit card and my $6K credit card and start an early-payoff savings plan for my $7K student loan balance. After just five days, I'm shocked at the amount of money still in my bank account, and I even survived the new Nordstrom catalog. Our three-year-old has even helped out by picking out re-gifts for his friends!
—Jess

I am tired of worrying about bills, my debt is maxed out, and today is the day that I start making a change. Time to get real about my finances and take control. I suspect there will be times that I fall, but I vow to get up again and keep pushing forward. I am forty and I won't live like this anymore! —Andrew

I'm taking the pledge. It is time to start focusing on my own problems with money instead of avoiding it. I want to be a role model for my husband, friends, and family instead of being the person who isn't true to their words and actions. I have no money but spend as if I'm rich. I gladly take the money my mother gives me and spend it recklessly. I'm ashamed. No more. I want to pay off my student loan, and I also want to honor my mom by paying her back. I'm starting now. —Olivia

You will create the pledge yourself so that it feels true to your goals. You want to say, essentially,

My name is _____, I'm committing to getting out of debt and to living a debt-free existence! Not only can I do this, I will do this!"

Take a few minutes to write your Get Out of Debt Pledge. Include what you're setting out to accomplish and why you want to do it.

Often, I'll find myself reading through the Get Out of Debt Pledges that have been written on AndThenWeSaved.com. I soak in the determination, resolve, hope, and commitment. I can't help but think, "Holy crap. All of these people want to be better versions of themselves. They're making this happen." Seeing all the pledges is so incredibly inspiring, and they remind me why staying out of debt is so crucial. They also remind me that getting out of debt in the first place was a major accomplishment, and I can't let myself get complacent about it. I never want to be in debt again.

Finding the Folks Who Will Cheer You Along!

Some people are lucky to have a whole bunch of other people around them who are nonstop supportive of whatever they do. Maybe they're family members or just a great group of understanding friends or even coworkers. But others might not have a strong support system currently in place.

There are a few options for finding a support team who will root for you throughout the entire getting-out-of-debt process.

First, though, let's talk about who not to seek support from. Try to avoid negative people in general. Negative people suck. It's hard to move forward with anything positive or proactive in your life because they always want to drag you back down into the muck with them. They feed on and thrive from complaining and talking smack. They will tell you every single reason the Spending Fast is a bad idea, why it won't work, why you should try something else, and so on. Trust your gut on this one. The Spending Fast is indeed hard, but it's completely doable. You need to surround yourself with people who will build you up and reinforce your positive life choices, not help you wallow in the bad ones. You can do hard things.

You might face some vulnerable or lonely times throughout the Spending Fast, but you don't need the added grief of dealing with people who can't support you as you change your financial life. Focus on the mission at hand.

So where can you find the supportive, great people who want you to have the best life possible? Here are some ideas:

> **Online.** Technology is completely amazing. We're able to connect with just about any group of people that we want. Some places to find support online: the And Then We Saved Facebook page, the Personal Finance subreddit on Reddit, and the Shopping Addiction community on Reddit. On these pages people root for each other and give ideas on how to handle different situations. It's great to see how people can come together for the same goal of getting out of debt, and learn how to live in a new way.

Twelve-step groups. I know this one might freak you out a little bit, but hear me out. There are twelve-step groups for just about everything, and luckily, there are ones for debtors and overspenders. These are groups of people who have tools (often called twelve steps) that work, and they might be able to relate to you in a way you haven't experienced with other people in your life. There's an honesty in these groups that isn't found in other settings, and they genuinely want to support you. Be open to the idea and look for the similarities in your stories rather than the differences.

Friends, family, coworkers. Be sure to be honest and vulnerable with the people who are already in your life. Tell them what you need support-wise (we're talking encouragement, not gift cards!). When you explain to them where you are financially and ask for their help, you just might be surprised at who opens up to you and tells you they, too, are struggling. Seek out the people in your life who seem to have their financial lives in order and ask them what their secrets are. I bet they would love to tell you how they did it.

Joining a Virtual Community

I touched on the importance of community earlier, but here's a little bit more on why it's such an important part of the debt-reduction process. As the months wore on during the year of my Spending Fast, my friends and family had heard the ol' "I can't because of the Spending Fast!" excuse over and over, and the novelty that was there at the start of my financial experiment deteriorated a bit. It wasn't there to rally me as it once did. I realized then how important it was to have a group of supporters around me. Because of my blog, AndThenWeSaved.com, I was lucky enough to have people cheering me along, which led me to set up the And Then We Saved Facebook page. Readers can go there every single day to talk about the specific difficulties they're going through as well as to share their successes and amazing paying-off-debt stories.

If you don't have supporters in real life, you can definitely find them virtually. I found that when I talked to people and they didn't really get it, sometimes they'd say, "Well, just quit," which isn't really helpful when deep down I knew I wanted to keep going. I found that I needed to talk solutions to succeed. Continuing with the excuses was going to keep me in debt.

Someone who understands your goals and why they are vitally important to changing your life can be more helpful. Having a group of supporters means you'll be able to continue when you might have otherwise given up. You'll be able to gain strength from them when your motivation is lacking, and you'll be able to give support when you see someone else struggling.

Being part of a community with the single aim of getting out of debt basically gives you an automatic group of people who believe in you. The community becomes cheerleaders who will be happy along with you when you pay off a bill and who will encourage you every step of the way.

Rallying Your Partner, Friends, and Family to Get on Board

When you set out to change your life, everyone might not be as excited as you are about the idea. I pretty much just plopped the Spending Fast idea on my husband because I was so desperate to get out of debt. At first Aaron wasn't excited about the Spending Fast idea at all. Our initial conversation went like this: "Hey, I've got this idea. I'm not going to spend any money for a year, and I'm gonna start a blog about it!" While I saw the Spending Fast as the answer to all my problems, he saw it as a major buzzkill. Turns out, we were both right. Eventually, Aaron started appreciating the benefits of the Spending Fast when he saw how much debt I was able to pay off. He also began to understand that I wasn't completely switching up our lifestyle just to torture him. As I dove into the Spending Fast and shared my money-saving methods, he couldn't help but get on board too.

Luckily for Aaron he's a natural Saver. I have to fight my inner self with all I've got in order to be frugal, and he's like, "Nah, I don't need it. We can leave." And that's that. Cue me, jaw dropped and baffled that he can walk away from a chance to spend money so naturally and effortlessly. In most cases, though, convincing your friends and family that your new frugal lifestyle is a good idea can definitely take some skill and finesse.

What I've Learned from Telling People About the Spending Fast

When you tell everyone about your new frugal way of life, be excited about it! No one wants to see their friend or family member suffer, so if you have an attitude of "Life sucks! This is going to be terrible," they'll take your lead and go negative themselves. Doing a Spending Fast is hard and it's definitely not a snap-your-fingers magic lottery ticket, so your excitement can be tempered with a dose of reality, but showing a lot of enthusiasm when you explain it to your family and friends will go very far in terms of getting your loved ones on board.

Be honest. Tell your friends and family why in the world you want to do a Spending Fast. Do you want to buy a house someday? Do you want to stop living paycheck to paycheck? Do you want to have an emergency fund? Do you simply need the weight of debt to be lifted? Are you sick of living a lie and pretending you're well-off when you're anything but? Do you just want to see if you can do it? Do you want to take a guilt-free trip to Cancun to frolic in the sun and wiggle your toes into the warm white sand? Tell your friends and family what's up. Be honest and forthright and you just might be surprised who opens up to you about their own money problems. So many of us keep our financial lives a secret. We want to pretend everything is wonderful when really it's not.

Know that you're rocking their world, and likely your relationship with them too. For the longest time you've said yes to every invitation. You've been their shopping buddy, their vacation companion, and pretty much their go-to Spender pal. By saying, "I'm changing this part of my life," you're telling them that your relationship with them will be different from here on out (at least for a certain amount of time). That change may take some getting used to, and they may not be happy about it. They may even be threatened by the idea that your Spending Fast sheds a critical light on their own spending habits. But I'm here to tell you that up to a point it doesn't matter what they think. Stand your ground and be firm in your decision. You know why you made your decision to do the Spending Fast and take control of your finances, and that's good enough. You don't need to justify it to a single soul.

Help them see what you see. You envision a life of freedom, a life in which you have fewer possessions, and therefore a life in which you need less money to live. When you're not stuck paying off massive amounts of debt for crap you've already forgotten about, and when you're not wrapped up in the cultural pressure to have more, better, and bigger, you'll be free. When you do a Spending Fast, you're able to buck the wasteful consumer culture. Maybe you'd prefer to work a part-time job and have a life beyond an eight-to-five paycheck. Working for The Man forever isn't on many people's life lists, so if you can get the people you talk to about your Spending Fast to understand this, they'll likely see that you're onto something.

Give them time. Your new frugal lifestyle could be a shock to your friends' and family's system. Let them take in the idea and they'll likely come around to it, especially if you share your excitement and don't mooch off them. Mooching isn't cool (I learned that the hard way—more on that later).

The Spending Fast and Relationships

I naively thought that the Spending Fast wouldn't affect my relationship with Aaron, because we didn't share money and we didn't have any joint accounts. (When we got married he didn't want to share money with me because of my debt and spending habits, and I didn't want to share an account either because I wanted to spend money the way I wanted to. The whole idea of having to ask permission to buy something sounded antiquated and laborious, at best.) But while in the past we might have gone to the movies or out to eat, or to the mall just to wander around and see if we "needed" anything, the Spending Fast quickly put an end to that (more on this in chapter 7).

I constantly blamed my inability to go out on the Spending Fast, and then there was that super-fun mooching thing I started up (I wouldn't mooch off anyone else but Aaron because I'm thoughtful like that). So while our money was technically separate, our lives were anything but. And the way our relationship was affected ended up being the hardest part, in general, of the entire Spending Fast.

The Spending Fast got awkward with friendships, too. One time a friend wanted to get ice cream. I told her the usual spiel about "Blah, blah, blah, can't . . . Spending Fast," to which she replied, "Oh, I'll just pay for it." I quickly replied, "Thanks, but no thanks. I've got money, I'm just not spending it." And then she said, "Well, how about you do something for me, like draw me a picture or something and I'll buy you a cone." "Hmm, I could do that."

Initially I wasn't comfortable with monetizing the friendship in any way, but I was okay with exploring options for bartering or trading. I found that by being open to the idea I was allowing myself to consider more creative ways to be social, ones I wouldn't have previously considered. (This interaction prompted an idea for a whole new side gig for making additional money by creating "Extremely Unflattering Custom Portraits of People," which later morphed into "Custom Vampire or Zombie Portraits" that I would eventually end up selling on Etsy to make additional money to help pay off my debt faster.)

Many other times I got invited out to dinner and stuck strong with my standard reply. Most people understood, and some didn't, and I was okay with that too. I found that if I replied in a way that showed that it wasn't up for debate or discussion, most people didn't give me a hard time about my decision.

I realized that the root of any negative vibes I was getting from friends about the Spending Fast was that they just wanted to hang out with me the way we always had, and they didn't want me to be miserable. I mean, that's understandable—who wants their friends to suffer? So when I told them I made the choice to do the Spending Fast because it was going to change my life for the better, and that in a year I would be able to join them just like old times, they were able to see that it wasn't about putting myself through the sacrifices for nothing. They saw that I was doing something really good for myself, and that it wasn't a forever thing. By framing it in such a way, each interaction and turned-down invite got easier for all of us.

Since I really did want to make relationships with others a priority over material objects, I had to make the decision to ensure that the people in my life realized that they were still important to me, even more so than ever before. It was just a matter of redefining how we spent time together. No longer could we simply get lunch at the new place that opened around the corner. Now we had to be a little more creative. Instead of going to a restaurant like usual, we'd take lunch to the park, where we'd sit on a bench as I ate my lunch from home and my friend ate her takeout. Rather than taking friends out for birthday dinners, it meant making them a homemade cake decorated as awesomely as possible (I also had a lot of free time on my hands, since I wasn't out spending money at stores).

I listened more closely, made eye contact better, paid attention longer, asked more insightful and thoughtful questions, and generally tried to show my friends and family through my actions (as opposed to giving them material things) that they were incredibly important to me.

The result was closer relationships, and the people I loved found it much easier to get behind the Spending Fast idea. They saw that we could still be friends, but spending time together would be a little different than it had been before.

 Let's Do This!

❑ Write your Get Out of Debt Pledge and post it on AndThenWeSaved
.com, or keep it private if you prefer.

❑ Set up a time frame for your Spending Fast, including start and end
dates.

❑ Let everyone know about your intention to do a Spending Fast. Tell
them why it's so vital that you get out of debt. Tell them that it will
be a difficult process and you'll need encouragement along the way.
Share the time frame of your Spending Fast, so they'll know what to
expect.

❑ Tell friends and family that they can show support by not asking you
to go out to eat or shopping. If they insist on asking you anyway, they
can show support by not giving you a hard time for saying no.

❑ Like the And Then We Saved Facebook page, follow me on social
media (@annanewelljones), and join a Debtors Anonymous group for
in-person support.

CHAPTER 4

How Much Do I Really Owe?

Right now you're probably thinking, "If I had the money to pay off my debt, I obviously would have paid it off already. There's just no extra money." Not too long ago I thought the exact same thing. I believed I was buying only necessities, and after paying for rent, utilities, food, and transportation, there was nothing left over. I couldn't even imagine getting close to paying off my $23,605.10 in debt on my income as a courtroom clerk. I figured if there was any chance of that happening I would need a higher-paying job, I'd have to win the lottery (which I didn't even play), or a large bag of money would have to appear on my doorstep with a tag that read, "Honey, it's your lucky day." All unlikely possibilities, considering the state of the economy and the lack of money lying around. I didn't feel like I was living extravagantly at all. I wasn't making payments on a crazy-fancy car, taking elaborate European vacations, or even handing out full-sized candy bars on Halloween. Money came in and was gone before I knew it. There was nothing left to pay off the giant pile of debt that was haunting me at all times. I was hopeless and out of options. Or so I thought . . .

Luckily, I've found that you don't need some outside force to rescue you from yourself and your mistakes. You don't need a lottery win, an inheritance, or a chance encounter with a random pile of money to take control of your life. The secret to wiping out debt (and keeping it wiped out) is to crush autopilot spending habits, modify priorities, and pare down expenses. These actions are the trifecta that will quickly get you out of debt once and for all, and as a bonus, you'll need less money to live on, since you won't be subsidizing your debt every month. How will we achieve this goal? By doing a Reverse Budget to figure out where all your money really goes, by creating a Wants and Needs List to curb your spending, and by making a Debt Hit List and a Payback Plan—all of which will be explained later in this book—to guide you throughout your Spending Fast.

Found: The Money

You can't meet goals when you don't know what they are. And if you don't know where your money is actually going, you can't stop it from going there. It's absolutely crucial that you know how you are spending your money if you want any chance at crushing those autopilot spending habits forever. It's easy to think that you need everything you're buying, but you have to be honest about your spending to make any lasting changes.

I didn't like what I saw when I forced myself to really examine my spending habits. I was spending way too much money on *everything,* but especially makeup. I was buying lipsticks, blushes, and mascara as if I were a makeup artist in training. I also bought poorly made clothing by the ton. I fooled myself into thinking that I wasn't really spending that much on clothes, because what I purchased was inexpensive. And I spent money like crazy at the grocery store. In addition to staples like bread and milk, I was tossing other things into the cart that I obviously "needed." The running script in my head went like this: "Hmm, it's the new *Us Weekly*! What is Kim Kardashian's booty up to now?! And, oh yeah, while I'm here, I should get the lightbulbs for the fridge and an extension cord for the fan."

On some level, I can understand how this behavior may not sound so bad. Most of us have gone overboard at the grocery store, but we're usually buying food, and that's okay because obviously we have to eat. Also, I was buying my lipsticks at Target and Walgreens—it's not like I was dropping $35 apiece at the Chanel counter. And the clothes I was buying weren't expensive, either. Spending $11 on a top and $4.50 on a lipstick sounds reasonable. But my cute tops and blushes in every variation of mauve weren't onetime purchases. I was constantly accumulating more, because I believed in the American dream that says "more is better," and the more you have, the better *you* are.

Even though the items were not pricey individually, I really shouldn't have been spending *any* money, because I was in so much debt. Since I was charging everything I was buying, I technically wasn't even spending my own money. The money that paid for tops and lipsticks really belonged to the credit card companies. Every time I tried out a new shade of pink I was borrowing more money from creditors, rather than paying it back. All these seemingly insignificant purchases added up to a surprisingly large amount of money—money that could have been used to pay back my debt. Every unnecessary purchase was furthering my stay in the red.

Until I let myself see my money habits for what they really were (impulsive), and not how I had imagined them to be (reasonable and practical), there's no way I could have made any kind of change. How will you stop yourself from buying random crap every time you hit the grocery store if you don't see how that package of pens is just another thing you don't need and can't afford, and it's keeping you in debt? It won't happen. We're going to start doing the prep work so you can get a fresh and objective perspective on what's keeping you in debt. We're finally going to face some things that you've probably been working hard to avoid. It's time to get straight with your money.

Are You All In?

Reading this book is a really good indicator that you're ready to start making some changes. But deep down the only person who can know if you're truly ready *is you*. I'm like the personal trainer who doesn't bullshit you. I'll give you tough love, but I'll also help you find the strength to do those twenty extra sit-ups. When things get rough, you might hate me a little (or a lot), but in the end you'll thank me for that beautiful six-pack.

Now is the time to stop making excuses. If you're not willing to do so, the Spending Fast is not going to work for you. If that's where you're at, it's okay. Try some other methods for getting out of debt first, and if those don't work for you, this book will still be here! Desperation can be the perfect jumping-off point to a good Spending Fast. You must be ready to do what it takes. You have to want to go *all in*. Facing the realities of your habits and being willing to make the necessary changes are the things that will make getting out of debt different—effective—this time. I had to face the fact that I spent way too much money on some really ridiculous stuff (it gets worse than makeup and clothes). All my purchases seemed important and justified, but if I examined the thinking that went behind them, it was clear I had a problem.

Building a Reverse Budget

The Reverse Budget is one of my favorite parts of the Spending Fast, as the process is a real eye-opener. Have you ever wondered where all your money goes? And it's a true mystery because you don't really buy anything that you don't absolutely need? Like, your money goes only toward practical things such as home-brewing kits or urban-farming implements? The Reverse Budget will solve this mystery and show you once and for all where all your money actually goes each month.

The Truth Is in the Bank and Credit Card Statements

To get a completely honest, objective view of how you spend money, you'll need to pull the last three months of your bank and credit card statements. Online or paper, whichever you prefer, but if you choose the online version, print them out. Many personal finance experts advise people to start tracking their spending when they decide to get out of debt, but there's absolutely no reason to delay the process when you already have all the information available to you. Plus, it's entirely possible that you might subconsciously—or actually, consciously—skew your spending to make your habits seem more favorable than they really are once you start tracking your money. What we're looking for are your unskewed, unabridged, undoctored spending habits. We need to see you in your natural habitat, like a honey badger out in nature. What do you buy when no one is looking? Are you buying jeans in every wash, fingerless gloves, rounds of drinks for all your friends, or too many screen-printed T-shirts? *We need to know.* We're going to see what your inner Spender has been doing with your money over these past three months, and we're going to do this by making a Reverse Budget: a detailed document listing all of your purchases in that time frame. This process will help narrow down where your money is going and will reveal patterns and problem areas.

Getting Started

This process can take a couple of hours, so you need to set aside enough time before you begin. You don't want to rush. Arm yourself with snacks (that already exist in your house), a cup of coffee, and your favorite playlist. Get a notebook and pen. Gather the bank and credit card statements that you dug out or printed, and you'll be ready to start the process of accurately assessing where your money is going. (Note: Resist the temptation to type out this exercise on your computer. When you handwrite every purchase into your Reverse Budget, the weight of each purchase is felt more fully.)

The Categories

The Reverse Budget will feature all the same categories you would use if you were making a traditional budget. Write out the following words in a row across the top of your sheet. Then create columns for each category.

Housing
Food
Utilities
Entertainment
Gifts
Transportation
Clothing
Insurance
Medical/Dental/Vision
Debts
Miscellaneous

Record Everything

Start by reviewing every line on each statement, and as you go, list every single purchase in the appropriate column. Be sure to record *everything*. Even if, say, you're starting a custom wood furniture business, you must include your tools and supplies in the list. If the category you need isn't included in the list I provided, simply add it.

Slowly, your spending patterns will become obvious, and you may begin to feel overwhelmed. You might even feel like stopping all together. Or you might feel a wave of energy come over you (this happened to me) as you revel in the joy of taking action and gaining new insights. You might become alarmed to see that the Food column is taking on a life of its own, or maybe Entertainment is five pages long.

Use more paper if you need to, but do not panic. You've got this. The point of doing a Reverse Budget is to see where your money is actually going. If you notice you're spending half of the amount of your rent on Miscellaneous items each month, you've already figured out why you don't have more money to put toward your debt—a problem area has been identified.

What's Your Average?

Once you've gone through all three months' worth of statements, add up the numbers in each column and divide by three. This will give you the average amount you spend on that category per month. Using three months' worth of statements provides a good sampling over enough time to reveal spending patterns. We all know that unexpected expenses pop up some months, and other months there are hardly any. Three months will give you a solid, unskewed look at how you spend.

Problem Areas Revealed

I learned some very interesting things about myself after looking at my Reverse Budget. I thought that my love of clothes *could* be a problem, but I was surprised to find that my hankerings for Chipotle burritos was very out of hand. Also, my attraction to business cards was dragging me down. I had more business cards for my (then side) wedding photography business than I could ever hope to hand out. I was buying multiple sets of cards each month. If I liked a design, it was really easy to cite them as a "business expense," because, well, they were for my budding business.

My purchases from Etsy (a website for all things handmade and vintage) popped up in my columns as a very large weakness. Since I'm an artist myself, I love to support other artists, so it was easy to justify spending this money. While I reasoned that every purchase was made with care (and they were), the list of things I bought from the site make me sound like a tween on a sugar high let loose with hundreds of dollars at a flea market.

Here's a sampling of my purchasing offenses:

For my husband (then boyfriend): a wallet made of black and yellow duct tape, one stuffed mini-Sasquatch, and a small-scale paper rib cage featuring a lifelike dangling heart in stunning detail.

For myself: a hand-carved rubber stamp of a bear with a tuft of hair and a sweet little heart on his belly, many earrings, and various cake decorations that ranged from Kewpie dolls to tiny hot dogs to a family of miniature deer.

For my twin sister, Kelly: a print of twin sisters sitting in chairs and joined by their braids, as well as a print of twin owl sisters wearing floral prairie dresses with Peter Pan collars, their arms interlaced. Because, you know, twin stuff for my twin.

Perhaps the best-ever purchase went to my future brother-in-law's girlfriend, who happened to work at a dentist's office. She received a ceramic tooth pin with a moist-looking gum that made it seem uncannily realistic.

While the bulk of the items that I purchased from the site were gifts, the expense of them added up fast, and my bank account didn't give me any mercy for being generous to others. It's probably safe to say that my sister didn't really need both of the prints, and some might even say I was being excessive in my gift-giving. They would've been right. Faced with my buying decisions in black and white, each column overflowing from the page, I had to come to the conclusion that I really liked shopping, and I seriously enjoyed getting mail. And this was a terrible, terrible reason to spend money the way I was. Going through my Reverse Budget allowed me to see how wildly and impulsively I was parting with my money. It wasn't reasonable to spend so much of my income on eating out, business cards, and cake decorations.

But there was a bright side. I could now see patterns that I was unable to recognize before. I saw the sad details about where my money was going, and how much I was wasting. The bottom line: I was buying stuff I didn't need with money I didn't have.

Problem Areas, Handled

While it was a little embarrassing to see how much I was spending on burritos and quirky prints of twins, acknowledging my problem areas was an important part of my journey from Spender to Saver. Until I saw for myself how my love of burritos was keeping me in debt, I wouldn't have had a clue they were actually something I needed to cut out. It can be frustrating to admit that you do actually have problem areas when it comes to spending. It can feel harsh to tell yourself, "Okay, the three p.m. Coke Zero has got to go," but it's these little steps that can lead to big changes. All of these small actions, like refusing a burrito or a Coke, don't seem like much individually, but in combination they produce results. It's little things that got you into debt, and it will be the little things that get you *out* of debt.

It's hard to know what exactly constitutes an official problem area when you're looking to cut back and get out of debt. For my purposes, a problem area was defined as "an unnecessary expenditure that appeared in my Reverse Budget multiple times." It's possible that when you do your Reverse Budget you'll see loads of unnecessary expenditures—guitars, cocktail shakers, throw pillows, and so on. And those expenses have to go. I want to make sure you pay extra attention to those "repeated" expenses, the ones that have become habits. As everyone knows, habits can be hard to break. But for the purposes of your Spending Fast, it's really crucial that you get these particular bad habits under control.

When acknowledging your problem areas, it's important to keep your eye on the big picture: getting free of debt and living life on your own terms. While I definitely missed my burrito lunches, skipping them was an easy trade-off when I thought about how I could be living debt-free and even running my own business someday. Instead of continuing to spend money on the area you've identified as a problem, think about the following goals instead.

Live debt-free. Envision what you'd like to do with the money you're sending to credit card companies every month. Take a vacation? Start a small business? Buy a house? Go to culinary school? If planning for it keeps you focused on the big goal, write about it, draw a sketch of your dream house, make a collage, create a private pin board on Pinterest. Do anything that keeps you feeling positive and focused.

Build a healthy savings account. Imagine how secure you'll feel knowing that you're done paying off your debt and have a savings account with actual money in it. It feels amazing to know that if your car needs fixing, your job situation changes, or your dog needs surgery, you can manage it financially.

Have choices. Being debt-free means having choices. You'll be able to make decisions based on what's best for you, your career, your family, and so on, and you'll no longer be ruled by the idea that your paycheck exists just to tame those never-ending bills.

I don't buy a lot of stuff. You can ask my wife—I wear my jeans until there are holes in the knees and pockets, and don't buy new ones until my wallet is basically going to fall out. But I couldn't figure out why I didn't have more money to put toward my student loan. After doing the Reverse Budget, I identified a major problem area. Turns out I was spending over $500 a month buying lunch at work. Once I realized how much it was adding up to, it became much easier to get up early and pack leftovers for lunch. That $500 I was spending is basically like an extra student loan payment. —Pete

High Alert: Defeating Problem Areas Forever

My in-laws are actually a big inspiration for me when it comes to dealing with problem areas. Their problem area? *Christmas ornaments.* Even in the middle of July, they can't resist the lure of glittery, pint-sized, blown-glass versions of deep-sea divers or deli sandwiches. Because they've spent loads of money on their collection (and it *is* impressive!) and have received tons of ornaments as gifts, their collection has grown beyond what they're comfortable with. The joy of hanging them all on the tree has been overshadowed by the time it takes to carefully store and manage them. Even so, Christmas ornaments remain a big temptation for them.

To deal with this problem, they put out a request to family and friends that they were done collecting. They also realized that they have to stay out of Christmas decor shops, no matter what. Identifying a problem area is a big first step, and it means you have to put yourself on high alert. It's also important to think about what measures you will have to take to cut the problem area out of your life once and for all. Some steps include:

Identify triggers. Triggers are people and places that put you in temptation's way. An example could be a friend you always go to thrift stores with or a place that carries items you can't resist.

Make a diversion plan. Have a backup activity in mind for times you're tempted to go to a place that you know is a trigger for autopilot spending.

Create a "commitment device." To prevent your future self from rebelling against your current goal-setting self, have in mind a preplanned "punishment" to get yourself back on track if you fall prey to your problem area. Punishment ideas include: vowing to post your ill doings on Facebook or Twitter. Put aside money for each slipup and send an extra payment to your credit card company. Commit to doing an extra hour of volunteer work for every X number of dollars you spend on a problem-area purchase.

Are You Your Own Worst Enemy?

Most likely, you're acting as your own biggest enemy in ways you may not even realize. Don't self-sabotage. You've got to be on your own side. I used to go to stores during my lunch break, mindlessly drop $120, and come back to the office with bags full of stuff. In order to break this habit, I knew I had to make a plan for this time that I was always tempted to shop. I could have gone to the gym or taken a nice walk—anything to keep me out of stores. It turns out that the best option for me was getting busier at work. I asked for more tasks, and I organized *everything*, which kept me occupied and engaged. As I know now, for me, *boredom = spend all the money.*

The Numbers Are In

Now it's your turn, my friend. What are the numbers in the columns telling you? Have you been spending impulsively? Mindlessly? Do you really need everything you've been buying? Are you surprised by any of the amounts? When I finished my Reverse Budget I couldn't help but feel pretty low about most of the choices I'd made. But here's the thing—those choices are in the past. The scary truth about my spending madness actually put me in a perfect state of mind to stop the chaos. Instead of rolling around like a fat, happy pig in the mess I had created, I used my frustration as the fuel to make changes. The catalyst was sparked.

Until I did the Spending Fast, it was almost as if I was on a mission to be in complete denial and utterly unaware of the true state of my finances. Since my debt symbolized demoralization, pain, and even hopelessness, I did everything in my power to avoid tallying it up or really dealing with my finances in any truly productive way. Think about setting up a budget? Gross. Talking about a 401(k) with Human Resources? I don't think so. The idea of deep-cleaning an oven covered in twenty years' worth of baked-on goulash sounded more appealing than thinking about fiscal responsibility. I thought, *Why deal with that boring, tedious stuff when I could just avoid it completely?*

For the most part, this had worked for me in its own depressing way. Before the Spending Fast became my plan I just continued to kind of deal with my debt as little as possible. I'd continue to pay the minimums, and, somehow, eventually, maybe by the day I died, my debt would get paid off. This was my "plan" up until that moment on the plane when I hit my financial bottom.

While You're at It, Get Your Credit Score and Credit Report (Yeah, They're Two Different Things)

Another exciting benefit of doing a Spending Fast is that your credit score will go up (this is actually really important, so go ahead and get excited). While most people can instantly tell you how many Facebook friends or Instagram followers they have, there's a good chance they're clueless about their credit score. When I was in debt I didn't know what my credit score was, either. A credit score is a number assigned to your credit report that indicates to potential lenders how big a risk it would be to let you borrow money. It's really important to know your credit score, because it can affect many areas of your life, not just whether you'll get approved for a loan or a credit card. A low credit score will impact your interest rate, and a high interest rate forces you to give more of your money to your creditors, leaving you with less money to live on.

Looking for a more exciting job opportunity? Then you really need to make sure your credit rating is decent. It's controversial, but more and more employers are checking the credit scores of job candidates. According to CNN, a credit score can be used to compare two candidates for the same position. You may be a perfect fit for a position, but if you're neck and neck with an equally qualified candidate who has a perfect credit score, you might get passed up. Get your number so that you can take action to improve your score if needed. This will be a big help whether you're applying for a loan or you're up for that dream job.

Your Credit Report

A credit report includes all of the details that make up your credit history. It provides information such as where you live, whether you pay your bills, how you pay them, if any accounts under your name were passed on to a collection agency, if you've opened any lines of credit recently, how old your loans are, if you've ever been arrested or sued, or if you've filed for bankruptcy. Also included on the report are court judgments and tax liens. It's important to check your credit report for inaccuracies and fraud from identity theft. If your report shows that you have an account in your name at Kohl's but you've never shopped there, you need to get the situation straightened out quickly.

You can request a free copy of your credit report once a year from www.annual creditreport.com. Just a warning, there are a lot of shady-looking credit score sites out there, so try to steer clear of them. There is absolutely no excuse for not getting your annual credit report, because it's free. The Fair Credit Reporting Act (FCRA) requires that each of the nationwide credit reporting companies, including Equifax, Experian, and Transunion, gives you a free copy of your credit report once every twelve months. Get in the habit of reviewing your annual credit report just like you take care of your health: Dentist, check! Physical, check! Credit report, check!

When you are ready to order your credit report, it's good to be prepared. Be ready with your social security number and previous addresses. Know that to verify your identity, you will be asked to answer questions that only you can answer, such as the amount of your mortgage payment or what street you lived on ten years ago.

If You Find an Error

The Federal Trade Commission (FTC) gives the following advice: "Under the FCRA, both the credit reporting company and the information provider [that is, the person, company, or organization that provides information about you to a credit reporting company] are responsible for correcting inaccurate or incomplete information in your report. To take advantage of all your rights under this law, contact the credit reporting company and the information provider." For step-by-step instructions on how to dispute credit report errors, go to the FTC website, www.ftc.gov, and search for "disputing errors on credit reports."

Credit counseling involves educating a person on debt and budgeting with the goal of reducing and eliminating debt. Credit counseling does not negatively impact your credit score if you just talk with a counselor and figure out a plan.

Debt management happens when a company takes over your accounts for you. You stop paying your creditors, and instead you make a lump monthly payment to the debt management company. Then the company distributes the funds to your creditors. Debt management can negatively impact your credit score because it involves closing accounts. Your credit score is calculated by using many factors, one of which is the average age of accounts. *U.S. News & World Report* states that "If you're relatively new to credit, it's best to keep your oldest card open, especially if it has a positive payment history. Closing it can hurt your score more significantly than it would for someone who has a much longer credit history."

Many sleazy companies out there are ready to take advantage of people who are in vulnerable positions. If any company tells you that they have secret strategies that aren't available to you on your own, if they advertise as being an "alternative to bankruptcy," if they require you to pay up front without providing basic resources to you, or if they hide their fees, do not go any further with them. These are four honkin' big red flags that you're on the path to getting scammed.

Before you give any personal information to a company, check them out through your state's consumer protection agency and the Better Business Bureau. Even better? Use one of the approved credit counseling agencies provided on the US Department of Justice website, www.justice.gov/ust/eo/bapcpa/ccde/cc_approved.htm.

Remember: You can set up payment plans and negotiate lower interest rates on your own without paying yet another company money.

Facing the Big Number: What Do You Owe?

It can be scary to face the figure representing your total debt, but you're not going to decimate it if you don't even know what you owe. It's important to note that for our purposes, debt is "the state of owing money." That means you're going to list any amount of money you owe to anyone, no matter how large or small it is. And it doesn't matter how close or how far you are to paying it off. Include *everything*.

List and Total Up Your Debts

Start by listing the kind and amount of each of your debts. Here are common debts you'll want to make sure to include:

Credit cards

Educational, car, bank, gas station, department store, tax, 401(k), payday, and furniture loans

Personal loans (money you've borrowed from parents, friends, relatives, coworkers, or business partners)

Overdraft account

Back child support

Unpaid bills (medical, dental, eye care, utilities, gas, electric, water, or any others)

Back taxes

Home equity loan and/or second mortgages

Mortgage

Once you have all the debts compiled, add them up so you know the total amount of debt you have. It's kind of embarrassing to admit now, but when I was buying all that stuff and accumulating debt like crazy, I had no idea how much it all actually added up to. If I didn't *really know*, I didn't have to worry about it. By the time I gathered the courage to tally up my debt (the estimate in my head of how much debt I had was under the real total by literally *thousands* of dollars, by the way), I was shocked by my number. I had to face the fact that the situation was way worse than I thought it was—and I realized there was no question that I needed to do a Spending Fast *immediately*.

A QUICK WORD ABOUT MORTGAGES

Many people don't include their mortgage on their Debt Hit List (which I'll explain in chapter 6) because it's one of those so-called "good debts" that you get fifteen to thirty years to pay off, plus it's also usually *massive*. It's up to you whether you want to include your mortgage. And just because it's an acceptable kind of debt to carry over a long period of time doesn't mean paying it off sooner than the time allowed isn't a great way to save you a ton of money in interest.

Find Your Interest Rate

Now that you've listed all of your debts, look for the interest rate on each of your bills and write it down next to the corresponding debt. Usually the interest rate will be right there on the bill, in plain sight. But if you're anything like me, you may have let your eyes completely glaze over the interest rate each time you opened a bill. If for some reason you don't see the interest rate visibly listed, you'll need to either log into your account online or call the credit card company to get that information. However, hold off for a second if you do need to make the call, because you'll also want to talk about something else that we're going to be discussing next.

Hello, Creditors: Renegotiating Your Rate

Credit card companies have big fees and giant interest rates for a reason: to make obscene amounts of money off their customers, which makes them evil, obviously. So you should call the customer service number for each of your credit cards and ask to have your interest rate lowered. First grab that interest rate information you gathered already. To keep you motivated, think about this: Creditors make their boatloads of money by giving you a loan and charging you interest. With every late payment or nonpayment, you accumulate more interest, and someone at your credit card company is in a plush corner office doing a happy dance. From now on, *no more* happy dances for creditors. Since credit card companies make the bulk of their money from late payment fees and the cumulative interest on your purchases, you're probably thinking, "Why would they want to help me?" or "Why in the world would they give me a better interest rate?" Here's why: Credit card companies are *a business,* and businesses *need to make money.* That's their *thing.* If you can't afford to make your payments or if you threaten to close your account (though as we discussed, you don't actually want to close your credit card account—doing so will hurt your credit score), they aren't making money. It's advantageous for them to work with you.

A few things to keep in mind while negotiating a better interest rate:

Be honest. While your tale of woe won't help, being honest about your situation might. As I just said, the creditors are a business, and they'd prefer to have *some* money rather than *no* money.

Be direct, calm, and polite. Simply explain that you would like a lower interest rate, and do it in a nice way. You'll get further if you're not rude.

Be assertive but realistic. Make "They want my money" your mantra during this process. Use that knowledge to your advantage to project confidence. Pump yourself up prior to the call by doing a few jumping jacks or boxing punches. Have an ideal interest rate in your mind, but don't disclose it. They might offer you a better rate than what you have in mind. Even the tiniest reduction will be helpful.

Be persistent and a little pesky, if needed. If the first person gives you a prompt no or tells you that you already have the best rate available, ask to speak to a supervisor. A higher-up will have more power and may be able to authorize a better rate. If the supervisor resists, ask, "Are there any actions I can take to get a better rate?"

Move on. If you can't get the first company to agree to give you a better interest rate, fine, you tried. Move down to the next one on your list—you're going to see success in some places if not others.

Wait six months and try again. If you tried everything and still couldn't get a lower rate, work on improving your credit score. After six months, get out your list and try again.

Now that you've gotten on the phone with all your creditors and asked for a better interest rate, you've already started to make a positive impact on your total debt payoff amount! #impressed

Don't Like Your Due Dates? Move Them.

There's nothing worse than having a bill due at an undesirable time of the month. When I was doing my Fast I worked as a clerk for the state, and we got paid on the last day of the month. One time a month. When I first started the job I couldn't wrap my head around how getting paid once a month would work. Having that one paycheck meant that every month, the day before I got paid, I would get out the stamps and envelopes and pay my bills all at once. I was able to save time by consolidating the task, I was able to track my bills easily, and I was able to get a clear picture of where my money was going. I called every company I owed money to and arranged to have the due dates on my bills switched to mid-month, around the eleventh. This date ensured I had enough time to get the bills out the door and avoid late fees.

Having due dates scattered all over the month can feel very chaotic. Consider moving your due dates to either the same date or, if you get paid every two weeks, split your bills into two groups so that you owe roughly the same amount for each pay period. Then set one due date for the first set of bills and a later due date for the second group of bills. Deciding on due dates for your bills is one more step toward taking control of your debt. You control your debt—your debt doesn't control you.

Prepayment Penalty? That's Nuts! Yes, I know.

Sometimes creditors will charge a penalty for prepaying (often 2 percent of the amount you borrowed). Once you get going with the Spending Fast, you're going to be throwing large sums of money at your debt, so you don't want any surprises. Find out if you would get penalized for overpaying any of your bills. If so, you'll have to change your Payback Plan (which I'll explain in chapter 6) slightly to avoid fees.

Here's what you should do if you're going to be penalized for prepaying:

See if you can renegotiate your contract so you can have **simple interest** (this is interest calculated based on the amount you still owe). This type of interest works in line with my philosophy that the faster you pay it off, the less you'll end up paying.

If you can't renegotiate and are stuck with **precomputed interest** (a fixed amount of interest that's predetermined at the start of the contract), then pay the minimum amount you are obligated to pay.

The money you have left at the end of the month after paying the top debt on the Debt Hit List will now go toward the next **non-prepayment-penalty** debt on your Debt Hit List. If you're wondering what the heck I'm talking about, you're going to be making a Debt Hit List soon. I'll walk you through the process in chapter 6.

Be sure to talk to the company that holds your debt, because they may have a specific way that you need to address an overpayment. Likely, you will have to specify if you want the extra money to go toward the principal or the interest. You want it to go toward the principal. It's reasonable to assume that if you overpay, the next statement will say that you owe $0, even though you still have a balance. *Send money anyway.* Remember, by paying more than what is due each month, you help yourself out by having to pay less interest over the course of the loan. This, we like.

A Little More Housekeeping

You've already done an amazing job of diving in and dealing with your finances. It can be a pain, but it feels so good in the end to have these things under control. There are a few other tasks I highly recommend you deal with now that you're all about financial well-being. Don't worry, none of these things will hurt.

Tell Autopayments to Take a Break

There are certainly advantages to setting up autopayments for bills (for example, you don't have to think about them), but that's also what makes them not so great (again, you don't have to think about them). For purposes of the Spending Fast, which is going to involve tracking your money very carefully, it's best to pause any autopayments until your Fast is over. I found that by having payments automatically transferred from my account, I was far less conscious about the money that was leaving my account. Plus, since we're in the process of instilling good financial habits into *the core of your being,* I'm going to encourage you to make a point of always checking your bills and statements for mistakes. If a company already has your money, they will be less inclined to work toward a speedy fix if you find an error. (Note: I'm all for making electronic payments in general. Online payments are fast, easy, and free—no stamps. But during the Spending Fast you're building money consciousness, not gliding through your finances in a half-comatose state, as you were doing before. Now you care if you're getting overcharged by $1.25! After the Fast you can turn the autopayments back on.)

Evil Overdraft Protection

Overdraft protection causes way more problems than it solves, by building up fees, allowing more debt to rack up, and carrying hefty interest rates. My overdraft protection account and I used to be BFFs, but not anymore. Overdraft protection is not your friend. You're going to start your Spending Fast by removing overdraft protection. Here's why: Many banks have a feature in which if you overdraft your account, they'll pay for the purchase anyway. The bank says that they do this to "save you the embarrassment of having your card declined," so they cover the purchase. You think all is good; then you get a letter in the mail saying that you're getting charged the cost of what you purchased along with a fee. This fee is typically $25 to $30, and it's how people find themselves paying $30 for a coffee at Starbucks.

Really, I couldn't care less about having my card declined. If I don't have the money, I shouldn't be making purchases. I'd much rather have my card declined than pay $30 for a cup of coffee. I would highly recommend finding out if your bank follows this practice, and if they do charge an overdraft fee, have the overdraft protection removed.

Automatic Deposits

If you haven't already, set up direct deposit for your paycheck. This ensures that your funds clear right away, and it's obviously easier to deal with than getting a live check, because you don't have to go to the bank to make a deposit or even add the task of making a mobile deposit to your to-do list.

Consider a Credit Union

Credit unions are member-owned nonprofit institutions that do the same thing your bank does. One of the nicest benefits of belonging to a credit union is that since they aren't out to make money off you left and right, you won't even be charged fees for using your ATM card. It sounds crazy, but some credit unions will actually pay you for using your debit card. Bananas! If you're planning to buy a home, you can still get a mortgage from a credit union, and the fees may be lower than those charged by a traditional bank. While it's getting easier to find a credit union you can join, know that often they are open only to employees of a particular company or members of a certain association. If you find you're repeatedly paying fees to your bank (the worst!), it's definitely worth researching if there's a credit union you can switch to.

Let's Talk About All This So-Called "Good Debt"

Lucky are the few that get out of college with no educational loans. For those with parents who covered the bill (or part of it), I hope you've written your parents a long letter of thanks. Educational loans are a major source of stress for many people, but especially for those who've just graduated—and especially in a rough economy. For college graduates who are a little further along in life, it's definitely difficult to still be making those payments each month, once you add in house payments and kid-related expenses. So, ultimately, how good can this so-called "good debt" really be? In a 2014 report titled *Are College Students Borrowing Blindly?*, Beth Akers and Matthew M. Chingos (both fellows at the Brown Center on Education Policy at the Brookings Institution) found that:

> *About half of all first-year students in the United States (based on nationally representative data) seriously underestimate how much student debt they have, and less than one-third provide an accurate estimate within a reasonable margin of error. The remaining quarter of students overestimate their level of federal debt.*
>
> *Among all first-year students with federal loans, 28 percent reported having no federal debt and 14 percent said they didn't have any student debt at all.*

U.S. News & World Report states that student-loan defaults are at 13.7 percent, but it's not just recent graduates who are defaulting. People tend to think of student loan debt as just a young person's problem, but that's not the case. According to *Tech Times*, about $18.2 billion dollars of the $1 trillion owed in federal student loans is owed by Americans age sixty-five and older! Who wants a debt, even an allegedly good one, hanging over their heads at age sixty-five? I think education is worthwhile, but taking out massive loans to pay for it—not so good.

I get it. I've been there. It's not particularly easy to finance a college education when you've just graduated from high school. When you're eighteen and signing your name on those financial aid papers, it's hard to imagine that in just a few years you'll be expected to start making monthly payments on gargantuan loans. As you might imagine, student loan debt is something I hear a lot about from my readers.

"It was a necessary evil to help me reach my life goal of finishing school."

"I have serious student loan debt and can't find a job that pays enough to justify my education costs."

Since I was in the same boat not too long ago, it's important for me to say that while I'm not suggesting you feel bad about financing your education, it's definitely in your best interest to pay off education debt as soon as possible. (*Duh*, right?) And that's where the Spending Fast comes in. Student loan debt is overwhelming, but know you're far from alone in dealing with that large bill.

Here are just a few tips for those of you who are struggling to make your monthly payments on educational loans:

Don't ignore your loans. Pretending they don't exist won't make them go away. Trust me, they won't take the hint. I tried it. In the end, ignoring them will just make everything worse . . . *as I know you know.*

Communicate with your lenders. Remember, they want their money back. Ask them for solutions to the repayment problems you're experiencing.

If you straight up just can't make this payment, apply for a forbearance, which is typically a short period of time where you're not paying the loan, but interest continues to accrue. I used one shortly after I graduated from college, and it was a good way to deal with a rough patch.

Look into income-based repayment. There are many programs available (especially if you work for the government or in a public sector that offers income-based repayment programs). Be sure to do your due diligence and ask your lender what options are available to you.

Research loan forgiveness and discharge plans. Loan forgiveness programs are a godsend. Depending what industry you're entering you may be eligible for one. A few options to look into:
- If teaching appeals to you, there are some student loan forgiveness programs available. You can't currently be in default, and there's a cap on how much is forgiven.

- For those in the public service or nonprofit sectors, some of these positions allow for debt forgiveness after 120 qualified loan payments. Get set up with an income-driven payment plan so your payments can be lowered as much as possible during the payment period. Visit https://studentaid.ed.gov/repay-loans/understand /plans/income-driven for more details.
- Each branch of the military has its own loan forgiveness program, and the amount forgiven depends on the rank you achieve.
- Both the Peace Corps and AmeriCorps offer forgiveness program incentives as well.

You're not going to find any program that magically erases your debt, but if you always planned to be a teacher, or if your grandfather was in the military and you've already been thinking about following in his footsteps, then definitely explore these options. Moral of the story: Don't leave free money on the table.

Consolidation

The quick-and-dirty definition of consolidation is "combining your various loans into one big, piping-hot, delicious loan stew." If you have federal loans (the kind taken out from the US Department of Education), you're allowed to merge your various federal loans into one loan. Afterward, you'll make only one payment each month, and the amount of time you have to pay the loan back will also likely be extended. There is *only one way* to consolidate your federal student loans, and that's through the Federal Direct Consolidation Program. If some company calls, e-mails, or even texts you saying that you can use them to consolidate federal loans, it's a scam. To find a safe place to consolidate, go to www.finaid.org/loans/privateconsoli dation.phtml for a list of credible lenders. Also, never prepay for the best rate when consolidating a loan.

Private Student Loans

I know you were wondering, *But wait! I have private student loans, too. Can I consolidate them with the federal ones?* Sadly, the answer is no. You can't consolidate federal loans with private student loans, because the federal government gives you a better interest rate than the private lenders do. Private student loans don't compete with government loans in the price department, so if you do consolidate your private loans, doing so will just make life easier by giving you one monthly payment. That being said, the consolidation process resets the term of the loan, so this may reduce the monthly payment. Just keep in mind, as with any debt, the longer you take to pay it off, the more you're paying in interest. So while that lower monthly payment may seem tempting in the moment, it may bite you in the ass in the long run. Be sure to do your research and calculate final payoff totals with each option.

But Wait! If Your Credit Score Is Improving . . .

Interest rates on private student loans are based on your credit score, so it's possible that you can get a lower interest rate via consolidation if your credit score has really improved since you first took out the loan. If you're about to start your Fast, it's possible that your credit score isn't all it can be. Because of the Spending Fast, your credit score is going to be getting the biggest makeover of its life. Keep in mind that if your score improves by about 50 to 100 points (or more—think big!), you might qualify for a lower interest rate if you consolidate with another lender. It's also possible that you can renegotiate with your current lender when your score improves.

It takes a long time to build a great credit score. The bummer is that it takes only a few minutes and one bad choice to totally destroy it. When I asked you to find out your credit score earlier in the book, I also had you pull your credit reports. Remember to check all this information *once* per year, perhaps as part of an annual financial spring cleaning. As I explained, the top three credit reporting agencies are required under federal law to give you one free report per year, and I want you to take them up on it.

A Bankruptcy Is Not a Free Ride

I'm not going to get into the many reasons to avoid filing for bankruptcy, but I will tell you that student loans are *forever*. Even if you were to get into a situation where you felt that filing for bankruptcy was your only option, you'd still have to pay off those student loans. It's really important that people understand this fact when they take out educational loans—whether you are using the money for a bachelor's degree, law school, or that master's in fine arts you've always wanted, you're going to have to pay it back, no matter what. Take the time to think about how much you're borrowing, and if the degree you're pursuing is going to lead to job opportunities that will enable you to earn enough to make the monthly loan payments.

Is College Worth the Expense?

Education is wonderful, and a college diploma may open a few doors, but is it the key to everything? If you haven't obtained a degree yet or are contemplating graduate school, you may want to think twice about it. Former New York City mayor Michael Bloomberg once said that high school grads should consider learning a trade rather than going to college. Comparing pursuing a trade with going to Harvard University, Bloomberg said, "Being a plumber, actually for the average person, would probably be a better deal. You don't spend . . . four years spending $40,000 to $50,000 in tuition without earning income." He may have a point. Bill Gates, Mark Zuckerberg, and Mary Kay Ash (of Mary Kay cosmetics) did all right without degrees. And here are a few more success stories to inspire you:

- Stacey Ferreira, who started mysocialcloud.com (a cloud-based bookmark and password vault), dropped out of New York University. She saw a tweet that a $2,000 donation would get her invited to cocktails with Virgin mogul Richard Branson. She borrowed the money from her parents. Branson was so impressed with her idea for the cloud vault that he ended up investing in her company.

- Matt Mullenweg, who started WordPress, dropped out of the University of Houston.
- Arash Ferdowsi dropped out of MIT to start DropBox.
- David Karp, who started and is the CEO of Tumblr, didn't even graduate from high school. Karp dropped out of Bronx High School of Science (that's a super-good high school in New York City) and now runs one of the most popular sites in the world.

PayPal cofounder Peter Thiel claims that college isn't necessarily worth the cost in the age of the Internet start-up. He believes this so much that he once gave twenty people $100,000 each to skip college and start companies. Sounds awesome, but you might want to think carefully before dropping out of college to sleep on a futon in a Palo Alto incubator. According to the Business Insider, while some people who did Thiel's program felt they "learned more about their abilities and the business world than through a college education," others dropped out. One participant said the experience felt "isolating" and made it "hard to meet people the normal way." So for some people, college may be just the thing. The people I mentioned in this section are wildly successful, and that's inspiring. But what about us regular people who haven't been coding since the age of five? Is college worth it? Economist Steven Levitt, of *Freakonomics* fame, thinks so, as do I. He states that "Every year of education you get will translate into an 8 percent increase in earnings over your lifetime. So, someone who graduates from college would earn 30 percent more, on average, than someone who only graduates from high school." In fact, the income gap between those with only a high school diploma and those with a college degree has never been greater. If college is still worth it, if that's the path you want to pursue, but at the same time student loan debt has topped over $1 trillion, how are you supposed to reconcile all this information?

A College Degree, Sans Loans (or As Few As Possible)

There's no doubt about it, tuition is expensive—but there are ways to obtain that prized piece of paper without the giant debt that usually goes along with it.

Community College

The biggest pro? Cheaper tuition. You can take core classes while paying significantly less money. Another plus? You can experiment—*You know what, I've always wanted to learn Portuguese!*—and then change your mind completely the following semester, as many college students do. There are often more night classes offered at community colleges, so you can attend classes in the evening while still working during the day.

Go Part-Time

Colleges and universities tend to offer a lower rate for registering for a full schedule, and that's something to consider. However, if you're able to cover the cost yourself while working full-time and going to school part-time, doing so may be worth it in the end. You'd have to look at the cost of the tuition at the school you're considering, compare interest rates, and do the math.

Have Your Master's Paid For

Some programs (notably for teachers) will pay for your master's degree while you're working in the field. As a perk, some companies will pay for additional education once you're employed with them. Before you fork over the money for grad school, see if there's a way to get your employer to cover the tab.

Just Get Smarter

Learning and broadening your horizons are wonderful things to do—but not if it means you end up deeply in debt. If you're itching to learn more, take advantage of the following:

There are many sites offering free online courses. For example, EdX (started by a partnership from Harvard and MIT) offers free online classes from Harvard, MIT, Berkeley, and many other universities. Topics include biology, business, chemistry, computer science, economics, finance, electronics, engineering, food and nutrition, history, humanities, law, literature, math, medicine, music, philosophy, physics, science, and statistics.

Contact the university you want to attend. It may offer online classes for free.

Online resources abound. Teach yourself a foreign language by downloading and listening to podcasts. Find tutorials on every imaginable topic on YouTube.

Over age fifty-five? Many colleges offer free tuition to "mature" students.

Want to start a business? MIT's Sloan School of Management offers free classes online.

If you want to learn it, there's a free way to do so. Want to study ancient Greek and Roman history? Just take the time to research the amazing opportunities that are available to you at no cost.

₷ Let's Do This!

- ❏ Create a Reverse Budget.
- ❏ Note problem areas.
- ❏ List your debts and their corresponding interest rates.
- ❏ Call your creditors. Ask for a lower interest rate and move due dates if necessary.
- ❏ Turn off autopayments and overdraft protection.
- ❏ Find out if you will be charged a penalty for paying over the minimum.
- ❏ If applicable, weigh the pros and cons of alternative education as opposed to traditional schooling.

WANT: TOO MANY THINGS.
NEED: TO WANT LESS LESS.
— Erin Hanson

CHAPTER 5

The Wants and Needs List

My old way of thinking followed a pattern: If I wanted something, that meant I needed it, which meant I bought it. No questions asked. This cycle is exactly how I ended up with an impressive collection of canned pineapple chunks (to be known forever as the Pineapple Kick of 2009), ten black tops with every kind of sleeve imaginable, several pairs of insanely awesome shoes—and of course the accompanying load of debt. Not being able to differentiate between wants and needs is one of the biggest reasons people aren't able to direct more money toward paying down their debt. It's the biggest reason I didn't put money toward my debt, and it's why I was completely convinced there was just no extra money available to do so. It's easy to find things you want, and if you're confusing Wants with Needs (knowingly or not), you can easily keep spending money you don't have forever.

Pre–Spending Fast, I was obsessed with coats. At the time, I would have viewed new coats as a Need rather than a Want. It gets cold here in Colorado, where I live, after all. No way could I be happy with last year's coat—I believed I needed *at least* one new coat every fall and winter. My main concern was that they were cute—practicality and affordability weren't even a consideration. This meant I was pretty much always on the hunt for a great new coat. One year, my twin sister sent me a link for a coat from J. Crew that she liked. I instantly agreed. Something took over me and I was *obsessed*. Obsessed, I tell ya. Here's the thing with me and my sister: We both love clothes. My sister even owns a buy/sell/trade clothing shop in Omaha, Nebraska. So I take her opinion on clothing seriously. Therefore I believed I needed *that* coat, even though it was lightweight and totally impractical for a Colorado winter. It was also $225. At the time I was working at a bar and $225 was (and still is) *a lot* of money for me to spend. I told myself that it really wasn't that expensive in the long run, because I would have it for many, many years. It would basically be like the coat was paying *me* to wear it, since I'd be getting so much use out of it.

This super-cool coat that I desperately needed turned out to be wrong on all sorts of levels. It was huge, unflattering, and a weird kind of gray-brown (greige?) color that washed me out in ways I didn't know were possible. But I'm not a quitter— I was determined to make that coat work. I thought a smaller size was probably the solution, but it wasn't. In the end, I paid more than $200 to look like I was wearing a massive paper sack. I kept the coat because my sister said it was cute, and on some subconscious level, I wanted her to think I was cool, and having the coat meant I was cool. I can now see that this made zero sense. But this was how my brain worked at the time: I really believed I needed that coat. In retrospect, I know that my identical twin and I share more than the same genes and a passion for clothes. We share a love of spending money—and can really enable each other. It goes both ways too. I once suggested she buy a pair of pants sight unseen, mainly because I thought they were amazing and bonus, they were on clearance. That's how my sister ended up with a pair of olive skinny pants with huge floral upholstery knee patches.

My Wants and Needs List

Figuring out that many of my Needs were actually Wants was a key part of how I finally crawled out of debt. My Wants and Needs List served as my guide. The list kept me on track, and I found myself referring to it often when tempted to buy something. Every time I pulled out my Wants and Needs List, I was reminded of the mess I got myself into, and how badly I wanted to be debt-free.

Creating a Wants and Needs List to guide your spending is a key part of the

Spending Fast. I'll get into the specifics about how to do it shortly, but basically I made a list of all the stuff I *had* to pay for. I started with no-brainers like rent and then went through my Reverse Budget to see if there was anything I overlooked. It's important to know that for the purposes of this Spending Fast, Needs are defined as "the fixed expenses you are required to pay each month, as well as the essential items or activities that make you a happy, healthy, and unique individual." The second part of the definition isn't a free pass to label everything you enjoy spending money on as a Need. Sure, cashmere socks and expensive chocolate might make most people happy, but what I'm talking about here is taking the time to think honestly and carefully about what you *require* to live your best life.

Priorities, Priorities, Priorities

A really important thing to understand about the Spending Fast is that this is about you, not me. Just consider me a messenger telling you about this new way of life. Keep in mind that you don't need to save and cut back exactly the way I did in order to get out of debt insanely quickly. Your Wants and Needs List has to reflect the priorities in *your* life. Obviously, we all have some basic similar Needs—housing, eating, and so on—and those kinds of needs really can't be avoided. But in order for the Spending Fast to direct you to the life you really want to live, it's crucial to recognize the other Needs that make your life complete.

I went to a photography college. The summer between sixth and seventh grade, my sisters and I hijacked my dad's old 35mm Minolta camera to take "modeling" pictures that highlighted our best nineties fashions and sassy model looks. Photography has been a passion of mine ever since. Holding photography exhibits was definitely a must for me, so adding "photography exhibits" to the Needs side of my list was completely representative of where I was in my life. Photography is my passion, not some frivolous thing that I was going to feel guilty about. During the Spending Fast I was still able to create my exhibits (though I did evaluate my old exhibition methods to find ways to cut expenses and save money) and keep that part of my life thriving— even though the austerity plan had been implemented everywhere else.

Another item that showed up on the Needs side was hair dye. This item usually surprises people, because it's not a blatant Need the way housing is. This is another example of how I was able to mold the Spending Fast to work well for me. I didn't want to start looking too rickety during the Spending Fast, so hair dye was allowed simply because I felt it had to be. I knew I could manage without new lipstick, but that I'd feel really ratty if I wasn't able to color my hair. It's your Spending Fast, so you get to make the rules. Think carefully about your other Needs, the ones that make you an interesting and vibrant person. Lots of things that seem as if they could be Wants may genuinely be Needs. If you're a passionate cook and you're hoping to save money to start a catering business, going out to eat may very well be a Need for you. If you're a writer, books and magazines may not be a Want the way they may be for someone else. And while I'm super-supportive of your Needs, remember that labeling something as a Need isn't an excuse to justify expensive spending habits you don't want to give up.

Don't worry about being too detailed and categorizing every little thing beyond food, rent, and utility payments as a Need. Of course, make the list thorough, but don't stress out trying to think of every possible scenario that could come up in a year's time. Situations that you never thought about before will present themselves to you throughout the Spending Fast. When this happens, your Wants and Needs List will be a guiding light, helping you make decisions.

Here's what my Wants and Needs List looked like:

Needs (What I Have to Spend Money On)

Rent

Utilities (keep lights and water off as much as possible; set the thermostat at 68 degrees and wear a hat and long johns inside, if necessary)

Cell phone (without Internet access)

Food (from the grocery store, not take-out; no brand-name goods; in-season fruits and veggies; and only when I run out of items I already have on hand)

Gym membership (local, reasonably priced gym; exercising is important)

Health insurance

Doctor's office copays

Prescription medications

Photography exhibits (done inexpensively)

Car payment

Car insurance

Gas

Public transportation pass

Hair dye (I saved money by dyeing it at home)

Wants (What I *Don't* Have to Spend Money On)

Gifts

Coffee at coffee shops

Clothes (make do and mend!)

Accessories

Trinkets

Etsy items

New makeup

Eating out

Movies at the theater

New business cards

Bed linens

Towels

Newsletter e-mail service

Home decor

Professional haircuts

Music

Keep a few different copies of your Wants and Needs List around. I referred to mine frequently, and was glad it was easily available every time I was tempted to spend money. Keep one near your computer so you won't be tempted to shop online, keep a minicopy in your wallet, keep one in your car (helpful when you're tempted to get take-out), and definitely keep a copy on your cell phone. Use a photo of your list as your screen saver to keep your goal where you'll always see it.

Define Your Needs

Think carefully about what your Needs are. What are you required to spend money on? What items and activities are crucial to your well-being? Where is money being lost? What spending can you cut out to get to your goals more quickly? Once you're able to separate your Needs from your Wants, you'll think twice before plunking down money for some random item that you'll have forgotten all about by the time next week rolls around. The key is to focus on your larger goals, with debt removal as the first step and the foundation on which all your other goals will be built.

Before you start envisioning yourself as an old-school pioneer living off the land, know that the Spending Fast isn't about total deprivation. It's about creating the space to have the freedom to make decisions. The bottom line is: Your life doesn't have to suck while you're on the Spending Fast. Granted, it probably will suck a little, but it doesn't have to suck a ton.

The beauty of the Spending Fast is that it will be tailored to your specific life. While you can use my Wants and Needs List as a guide, your list might be totally different than mine, and it should be. Only you can deem what's important in your life, and your Wants and Needs List should be a reflection of your personal priorities and lifestyle needs.

Start with the Obvious

You'll start your Wants and Needs List with the most obvious Needs you have. Before I made my list, I spent some time thinking about all the bills and debts I needed to pay while also referencing my Reverse Budget. I made sure I included every obligation I had—loans to my parents, housing, food, and so on. I also had to think about things like bus fare. It's easy to forget how expensive it is just to exist. Make the task of listing your Wants and Needs easy. If you're paying a mortgage or rent, this item is clearly a Need because you need a place to live. You've also gotta eat, so food is another obvious Need. Go ahead and list all of your obvious Needs. And of course include all of the credit card bills you're trying to pay off, student loans, car loans, medical bills, and so on. Everything you're required to pay every month should be listed as a Need.

Ask the Survivalist Question

Once you've listed all of your obvious Needs, review every item on your Reverse Budget and ask yourself if each one is genuinely a Need or a Want. Separate Wants from Needs by asking yourself the Survivalist Question: *Is this absolutely necessary to survive, or not?* If the answer is no, then list the item as a Want. Most things will easily fall onto one side of the list. There will be plenty of items you'll know immediately in your gut that you can easily do without. You may decide you have plenty of socks to last you through the next year, or that last summer's bathing suit will still fit this summer. You might decide you'll stop spending money on expensive shampoo or on magazines. If you're stuck on a few, that's okay. I'll get to those gray areas in a minute. Here are a few clues that an item can immediately fall onto the Wants side of the list:

> It's not related to your passions or overall well-being.
> You can immediately think of a cheaper option or free substitute.
> Your roommate or family will let you use theirs.
> You can get it for free at work (without being shady about it).

Identify Your Gray Areas

The ones that fall in the middle—the things you're not sure you can go without but can't easily label as Needs—those are some tricky little beasts. One of the reasons I believe the Spending Fast worked for me is because I let myself have Needs beyond rent and food. While I can't stress enough that the Fast won't work if you don't cut back in a big way, I think that it's a mistake to cut out every activity or expense that makes you a happy, well-adjusted, interesting individual. But you have to be extra careful about those tricky items that may fall somewhere in between. For instance, a prime example of an expense that usually falls into the just-can't-decide-where-it-should-go area is the gym membership, even though most people would agree that health and fitness are important. Internet service and smartphone plans are two more examples of expenses that can be hard to categorize.

When I was creating my Wants and Needs List, I noticed that my Reverse Budget showed a lot of money was being spent at places I didn't even consider potential problems: movie tickets, gifts, and phone and Internet services. I could definitely eliminate trips to the movie theater (though my husband wasn't going to be happy about it). I could think about gift-giving in a different, more industrious way. Although cutting out restaurant meals would be an unwelcome change, it was definitely doable. Internet service was a need for me, but I had to get real with myself. While I had to have Internet access, I didn't need *the fastest Internet ever*. I realized I was able to get by with the slightly slower but cheaper connection. As it turns out, I was enjoying the progress I was making with my finances so much that after a month I asked my husband if we could get rid of our Internet service *altogether*. I argued that there was free Wi-Fi access at work and at the library. I also tried to convince Aaron that we could do without cable. He wasn't into either of these ideas, but I *was* able to convince him that we could (and should) go with a less expensive plan for both, so that's what we did. I was adjusting to my new lifestyle. I was discovering that I could get by with less, and I *wanted* to get by with less. Rather than complaining about what I was missing, I now thought: *What else can I cut out?*

What Are You Stuck On?

When creating your Wants and Needs List, take the time to carefully consider the items you are reluctant to cut out. Are you reluctant because a massive, life-altering chain of events would result, such as maybe not getting freelance work because you don't have Internet access? Or a total elimination of your favorite hobby? Or are you reluctant because it will be slightly awkward to tell your friends you've eliminated going out for cocktails for the foreseeable future? Deciding what your Needs and Wants are isn't about coming up with excuses or justifying expensive behaviors; it's about taking an honest look at what you really require to be happy at a basic level. These are tough choices. Here are a few things to think about when debating whether gray areas count as actual Needs:

> Do I want this material object more than I want to be out of debt?
> Is it 100 percent necessary to my job or overall sense of well-being?
> Is the *idea* of getting rid of this thing worse than actually cutting it out?

If after some serious soul- searching you're absolutely convinced that a particular expense is a Need, go ahead and put it on your Needs list.

After much debate, I decided to keep my gym membership on the Needs side of my list, even though it was a big expense at $120 a month. My gym is expensive because it offers two hours of free, high-quality child care each day. I knew that I could go to a cheaper gym, but working freelance with two little kids made it really hard to incorporate working out into my schedule. I forced myself to think about what benefits I was getting from the gym. Was it really worth the money? I was working out daily, my kids were loving the play space, I got a break, and I even had time left over to answer e-mails about various freelance projects before I had to pick up my kids. We also spent lots of time at the indoor pool, which was really great, especially in winter. It kept us from spending money on other activities. I realized I felt I was getting my money's worth out of the gym, and it was a really positive *place for everyone in the family. It was about physical health, community, mental health, and fun! Once I decided to put the gym on the Needs side of the list, I was more brutal about cutting out other things. I'm really glad I kept the gym on my Needs side. It kept me sane.*

—Emma

Your New Mantra: Do It Cheaper

The good news is that the gray areas often present an opportunity to save even more money—which is exactly what we're after. You might be surprised by how creative you can get. Is there a way to get one of your gray-area items completely for free? Consider other options that you may not have previously thought about. With my gym membership, for example, even though I decided to keep it on the Needs side, that doesn't mean that I had to keep paying as much as I had been paying. I got $15 off our monthly family membership by calling the manager and asking for a lower rate. It took less than five minutes of my time, and the yearly savings really add up. That's $180 saved right there.

While I'm obviously an advocate for Needs-Only spending, I've seen firsthand the changes that can be made when you try to do the stuff you love doing for less. Just because something is a Need doesn't mean it has to be expensive.

PURSUING MY PASSION: THE CHEAPER VERSION

I wasn't willing to put my passion for photography aside because of my debt— photography is too big of a part of who I am. After some careful examination of how I handled photography exhibits, it was clear I could prepare for them more cheaply than I had been without losing out on this important part of my life.

Everything was now under investigation, from the number of shows I did to how I presented my work. I didn't want to give up exhibits, so I got creative about how I used the money I did spend on them.

Photography Exhibits, Pre–Spending Fast

No limit on the number of exhibits I participated in each year.

In each exhibit I would show a large quantity of very big photographs on heavyweight photographic paper.

The size of the pieces I chose required custom frames and custom-cut glass.

I spent a fortune on promotional postcards and new business cards for each show.

I bought new clothes to wear to the openings.

If the show was out of state, I paid to ship the pieces to the galleries and tried to attend each opening.

I had no idea how much I was spending on each exhibit, and at the time, I didn't really care. When I did my Reverse Budget, it was eye-opening to see the costs tallied up. I ultimately wasn't making money selling my work at exhibits, but I convinced myself that this fact wasn't important. I was driven to do the shows for creative reasons, which was enough of a justification to continue. Once I created my Wants and Needs List and had to figure out how to do some of my Needs cheaper, I was shocked by how much I was able to cut back on.

Photography Exhibits, Post–Spending Fast

I was more selective about what exhibits I was a part of and chose to participate in only local shows.

I chose fewer pieces for each exhibit.

I opted for smaller prints in standard sizes (which reduced the cost of framing glass too).

I used cheaper framing techniques and took advantage of a frame shop's "buy one, get one for a penny" deal.

I stopped making card-stock promotional pieces and ran off a small quantity of copies at work instead.

I committed to one design for my business cards.

I put the clothes I already had together in new ways. No more new outfits!

Once I started seeing how much I was spending on exhibits compared to how much I brought in from sales of my work, making these changes was a no-brainer. Gallery shows became less appealing when I realized how much they were costing me (I admit that I felt like a bit of a schmuck when I figured this out). The good news is that I started applying for public art grants, and because I wasn't spending so much time preparing for exhibits, I had more energy to invest into me and my husband's wedding photography business, which has been far more profitable and fulfilling.

How Can I Do What I Want for Free (or Really Cheap)? Questions to Ask

Can I get free or discounted classes at the yoga or Pilates studio if they are taught by an instructor in training? If I clean the gym or studio, can I get a free membership in exchange?

Can I drop the gym altogether and start running outside? Is there a running club in my neighborhood (check Facebook groups)? Is there a cheaper gym nearby? Does my gym offer part-time memberships or scholarships? Can I pay per class? Can I get a discount for referrals? Will my health insurance reimburse me for part of the membership fee? Is there a low-cost neighborhood pool I can swim in for exercise?

Does the library have all (or most) of my media needs covered? Can I start a book exchange in my neighborhood? Does my library offer used book sales?

Can I do a clothing or accessory swap with friends? What about swapping kids' toys and books with other families?

Can I barter for the things I may need? Car repairs? Website coding?

Can I do marketing, copywriting, social media production, or something else for my favorite local restaurant to get an occasional free dinner? (Or many free dinners?)

Is there something I can offer in return for free child care? What about doing some child care yourself to offset the costs? Can I create a babysitting co-op where no money has to be exchanged?

What benefits does my employer offer that I haven't fully utilized? (I found out after four years of working for the state that I could have been getting a discounted rate on hotels and car rentals with my ID from work!)

Needs-Only Spending

Congratulations. After lots of thinking, pondering, and tough decision-making, you've committed to the idea of being a Needs-Only spender. I remember how it felt to know I'd no longer be going out to dinner with friends or buying any new clothes. I was simultaneously nervous and excited, and in the beginning, spending money on Needs Only felt easy. I was proud of myself for taking action and didn't initially feel tempted by Wants. But throughout the year, there were many times I was seduced by items on the Wants side of my list. I knew rationally that house decorations and new music were Wants, but that didn't always keep me from *wanting them*. After surviving over a year in Needs-Only mode, I have some tactics to help keep you from wandering back over to the Wants side.

When the Wants call out to you, you have to be ready to fight back. Here are some strategies that worked for me:

Refer to your Wants and Needs List. You're no longer a slave to your spending impulses. *You* are in control now.

Put a "pause" between you and the purchase. The pause gives you enough time to regroup and remember why you're committed to Needs-Only spending. Debt freedom, baby!

Call a supportive friend (do *not* text a picture of the item you're tempted by to the friend who will respond with "OMG, GIRL. YOU LOOK GOOD! YOU HAVE GOT TO HAVE THAT!!"). Text the friend who knows how crappy you feel about your debt. This is the friend who has your financial back and will tell you, "Girl. Get out of that store *right this minute!*"

Walk through the "Should I Buy It?" decision card (see page 128).

Keep "pleasure buying" at bay by keeping yourself fed, well rested, and exercised. Being hungry, tired, extra happy, super-sad, lonely, bored, envious, or stressed can activate the impulsive shopping response. Keep tabs on your emotions.

Avoid tempting situations like window shopping.

Okay, this sounds kind of cheesy, but it works: Make a Gratitude List. Every day, write down at least five things you're grateful for. Contentment comes from shifting your thinking from "what I want" to "what I have."

Keep yourself occupied. Look at the list of 151 Things to Do Instead of Spending Money on page 211.

Remember how shitty it feels to be in debt, and that by not spending money on Wants, you're actively on the road to getting out of debt.

Think about the reasons *why* you want to be out of debt: traveling, buying a home, having a family, having financial security, taking a guilt-free vacation, making dreams come true, feeling free, knowing you took on a challenge and nailed it.

Remind yourself that you're a lot stronger than you think you are. You won't be taken down by fabulous shoes, a new juicer, or a mean hankering for some frozen yogurt.

Study after study shows that the anticipation of having an item is more enjoyable than actually owning it. Focus on the fact that your current state of *wanting* is likely the peak of your enjoyment with the item.

(Almost) Anything Can Be Returned

I had pretty bad buyer's remorse. I'd buy something and immediately think, *Shit. I did it again. How did I let this happen?!* But oddly, an extra gift that came out of the Spending Fast is my newfound ability to return *anything*. I have no qualms about returning something I don't absolutely love. If I don't love it, back it goes. There's no limit to what I'll return. I've sent back lentils at a restaurant that I felt were too lemony (no way was I paying $4 for over-lemoned lentils). After reading a blog post on clockmaking, I decided I absolutely had to make a clock. Once I determined that in reality, this project wasn't going to happen, the stuff went back—even though the kit I bought was only $5.

While ideally you're sticking to your Needs list, if you accidentally buy a Want, *you don't have to keep it*. Keep the tags attached and hang on to your receipts. Once the adrenaline generated by the purchase wears off and you hit that oh-so-familiar spending shame mode, you can turn the situation around by returning what you bought. It's great that we can return things if it comes to that, but we all have way better things to do with our time than to continually buy things only to return them soon thereafter.

Hopefully you're keeping receipts handy (during the Spending Fast I kept mine stored in a large manila envelope in my closet; now I digitize them), so you don't get stuck with an item you don't need. Keep in mind that many stores are now able to look up a purchase if you paid using a credit or debit card. Target, Walmart, and Costco are just a few stores that will look up a receipt for you if you can't find your copy. Here are a few other tips about returning stuff that are easy to do and worth the effort.

Find out the return policy *before* you buy. You don't want to get stuck with something just because it's marked "final sale" and can't be returned.

If making a purchase online, shop only at places that offer free shipping *and* free return shipping.

Return the item as quickly as possible. Many stores require that returns be made within a certain amount of time, such as thirty days. You might be forced to keep the item if you hang on to it and let too much time pass, missing the return window.

Bring the credit card you used to purchase the item with you to the store. If you don't have the receipt, showing the card will help—and stores sometimes need your actual card to process the credit.

If you're stuck with store credit, make the best of it and see if you can use it for an item on your Needs List. Be sure to find out if the credit expires, and keep the voucher or card in a safe place so you'll remember to use it.

Just Cancel It

Once I started returning stuff with no remorse, essentially eliminating all the guilt I'd get from a purchase, I decided I would go even further and cancel things before they even arrived. I'd do this if I knew the item was something I shouldn't have bought in the first place. If you're shopping online and you feel regret after clicking PAY NOW, know that it's often possible to cancel the order. Not long ago I was thinking yellow shoes were a must for summer. Yellow shoes were *on my mind*. After I ordered the shoes, I realized that I was letting my Wants take over. So I canceled the order. While I'm pretty good about being a Needs-Only spender, to this day, there have been a few times where I've bought something and realized, *Wait a second. Back it up. I don't need that*. Don't be afraid to cancel an order.

Sometimes I'd place an order and then immediately think, *Why did I just do that?* I've been known to order a pizza only to call the restaurant up minutes later to say, "You know what? Never mind." I just couldn't see spending $22 for a meal that I would regret twenty seconds after I ate it, especially when I had perfectly good walnuts, hummus, yogurt, and bananas eyeballing me from the kitchen. Please note that while I'm all for being thrifty, I'm 100 percent against being a jerk. If you're going to cancel something like take-out, you've gotta do it right away. Just because you've changed your mind about spending money on pizza or Chinese food doesn't mean it's okay to stick the company with the bill for wasted food.

I've ordered some crazy things, but have learned to immediately turn the situation around by picking up the phone and canceling the order. I once impulsively ordered some fast-acting Lactaid pills after a particularly bloaty run-in with a bowl of chocolate ice cream. Canceled. I couldn't find one of the forty-seven baby bibs we own, so I ordered a new set. Canceled. I found that after I placed an order, I could take a minute to calm down and then go right back and cancel it. Throughout all this, I've learned that just because I occasionally fall back into my old ways, it doesn't mean I have to stay there. Just because I still act impulsively at times, all is not lost. It's always tempting to go for a quick fix when you hit a rough patch, but I've learned to mitigate the damage as best I can. I also try to think about how I could have reacted differently, so that the next time I'm frantically searching for a bib, I don't resort to buying something I don't need, only then to waste my time by having to cancel the purchase a few minutes later.

Developing New Needs Along the Way

You've gotta be careful about trying to take a gentler approach by suddenly developing new Needs along the way. One of my main goals with the Spending Fast was to stop focusing so much on material objects, and to work on developing healthy relationships with the people in my life. Early in the Spending Fast I was having a hard time finding ways to hang out with friends that didn't require spending money. Since working on relationships was something I identified early on as a goal, I decided that spending money to be with people was actually a Need that I had overlooked. Maybe I should give myself a small "allowance" every month to do so. I wrote a post for my blog about my predicament and was sure readers would respond with a resounding, "Yes! You definitely need a socializing allowance!" I was wrong. Nearly everyone who responded to the post said I should not give in. I was so glad the readers talked me out of it, because I had already managed to justify this new need to myself.

$ Let's Do This!

- ❑ Create your Wants and Needs List. Wants go on the left, Needs go on the right.
- ❑ Write down all of your obvious Needs.
- ❑ Refer to your Reverse Budget to ensure that you cover all of your expenses.
- ❑ Ask the Survivalist Question. Do you need a given item to survive?
- ❑ Identify your gray areas.
- ❑ Ask yourself, "What things can I do more inexpensively?"
- ❑ Spend on Needs Only.

i CAN DO HARD tHiNGS.

CHAPTER 6

Constructing the Debt Hit List and Executing the Payback Plan

You've just written out every detail of your debt. That takes a lot of courage, and I know from personal experience how overwhelming it can be to face that number for the first time. Stay strong—even if you've just come to the conclusion that your debt is bigger than what you earn in a year (or in multiple years), or if you've realized you missed a bunch of payments. You *can* do this. I've heard people say they can't possibly do the Spending Fast because it's just too hard—or that it will be impossible to make any headway. Do not give up before you get started. Freedom from debt is the most awesome gift you can give yourself. Before you start freaking out about how this is actually going to happen, know that we're about to make a Debt Hit List and Payback Plan. The Debt Hit List is the list that will show you the order in which you will pay back your debts. The Payback Plan is the process you will utilize to execute your Debt Hit List. With the Debt Hit List written out, you're going to have a handy blueprint you can refer to during every stage of your Spending Fast. The Debt Hit List will show you who gets paid the bulk from your Spending Fast efforts. With the Payback Plan you'll know exactly how to successfully accomplish your goal of paying off your debt and living autonomously.

Make a Debt Hit List

Create a new list that details each of your debts in order from the highest interest rate to the lowest. If you happen to have two debts with the same interest rate, list the smaller debt on the line above the higher debt.

The list you've just created is your Debt Hit List, and you are now Vincent Vega, complete with a bolo tie. You're going to target the debt with the highest interest rate first, gleefully crossing each debt off as you work your way down the list to the one with the lowest rate. It will feel mind-blowingly amazing every time you cross off a debt.

Let's talk for a minute about why we are tackling your debt from the highest interest rate to the lowest. The longer you have an outstanding debt with any interest accruing, the higher your final payoff amount will be, which can also mean it will take that much longer to eliminate that debt. You don't want to swim upstream any more than you have to, so it's best to avoid adding more debt to the stack by taking longer to pay it off. While it would feel nice to list the debts from smallest to biggest—it would feel deceptively good to pay off the small debts quickly, just because they're the smallest—you'd be screwing yourself over by doing so. Here's why: Compound interest is a bitch. With your Debt Hit List, you will pay the minimum due on each of the lower-interest-rate debts while the bulk of your money will be directed to the top debt on your hit list. You will be motivated and energized to continue with your Spending Fast because with each lump sum you're able to send to pay off your debt, your momentum will be building.

If you have a debt that isn't necessarily a top priority in the interest department but is weighing on you emotionally, go ahead and move it toward the top of the list. For example, my parents weren't charging me any interest on the loan they gave me, so initially that debt was at the very bottom of my Debt Hit List. Once I realized how much this debt was affecting my relationship with my parents, though, I shimmied it right up to the top. Sure, I paid a bit more interest on my debts overall by doing so, but it was important to me that my parents get their money back. They had already waited long enough.

Tracking Your Bank Balance

Use a basic blue-and-white paper checkbook register (get one free from your bank or download one for free from Google Docs) to input every penny that goes into or out of your bank accounts. Stock up, you're going to need quite a few of these registers throughout your Fast. The first thing you're going to write in the register is your *current bank balance*. I don't care if it's $5, or –$5; changing your habits starts with knowing how much money you really have. Over the course of each month, log every single credit and debit to your account. You'll also calculate your balance after making each entry. This tracking method is the primitive system our parents used in the days prior to *computers, smartphones, and apps.* At any moment I should be able to stop you on the street and say, "Hey, *exactly* how much money is in your account *this* second?" And you'll know the *exact* amount. Not "Oh, I think about $322? But wait. There's the automatic withdrawal for my cell phone bill, and I wrote that check for Girl Scout cookies. Hmm, yeah. I think I bought $40 of Thin Mints?"

Because you're being attentive, accurate, and vigilant with your finances, you'll also log into your bank account online to note when actual checks and bills have cleared. You're not using this step to learn how much you have in your account (because you already know); instead, you're checking that you aren't being overcharged (accidentally or otherwise) for any of your purchases or on any fees. As you look at your account online you'll also be checking to make sure that you haven't missed inputting any debits or credits into your paper register. Keep your receipts organized, so you can reference them easily if you have any questions about a purchase (or if you need to make a return).

We're Not Dealing with Budgets

I think you'll probably agree with me that the word *budget* sounds depressing as all hell. It really doesn't matter what you call it—a spending plan, a spending freeze, a no-spend year, a diet, a Fast! But for goodness' sake, please just don't call it a budget. Because if you're anything like me, you've learned by now that traditional, tedious budgets don't work. You'll want to think about the Spending Fast as a philosophy that you can apply to any situation that could come up. Following directions is helpful and it's good to have guidance, but the goal is to develop a new way of relating to money—so you'll have the tools to succeed even after your Spending Fast is completed.

I'm mentioning budgets here because the Spending Fast plan isn't about following a budget to the letter. The Spending Fast is *not* a budget. It's a strategy to use to develop a new, healthier relationship with money, one in which you have a general sense of approximately how much money you need to pay for your Needs as they come up. With a Spending Fast, you won't have to figure out exactly how many dollars to spend monthly (or weekly) according to categories such as food or transportation, which is how a traditional budget works. You won't be blowing every cent you have. You'll operate in a way that enables you to pay for what you *need*. And only for what you need. And with those needs, you'll be paying as little as humanly possible. If you follow the Spending Fast plan correctly, you'll have enough money left at the end of the month to pay your bills and you'll be able to send a large payment to the number one debt on your Debt Hit List.

The Spending Fast Cycle

During my Spending Fast I worked for the state of Colorado. It was a government job with a set salary. I was paid once a month, at the end of the month. From month to month each check would vary only slightly (plus/minus $50). Knowing I would have a predictable amount of money directly deposited into my checking account on the last business day of the month helped make for an easy Spending Fast cycle. No matter whether you get paid the same amount each month on the same day of the month or you have a sporadic, unpredictable income, you can make the Spending Fast work for you. The key is to decide on a Spending Fast cycle length. I recommend having your Spending Fast cycle be a month long, but it's up to you. If you get paid every two weeks you can choose to have that be your cycle length. Your Spending Fast cycle length comes into play with the Payback Plan when you start thinking about when you will pay the bills and when you will write out the check for the top debt on your Debt Hit List.

The Day Before Payday

Following the Payback Plan, you will write out the checks and prepare the payments so they'll be ready to send out the next day, once the paycheck has been deposited. This is done on the *day before your payday*. You want to be completely sure you know exactly how much money is in your account, and what purchases and expenses may soon be deducted, before you pay your bills (and other Needs) and calculate that month's payouts. Writing out your bills the day before payday also allows you to start with a fresh slate for the new pay period. We're going to zero out the bank balance, only to have it refreshed right away. Read on and I'll show you what I mean.

Calculating the Payout Money for Your Number One Debt

The payout money is what's left over after you've paid for all of the items on your Needs list. Every single penny that remains after you've accounted for your housing, food, and other regular bills—including the minimum monthly payments for each of the lower-interest-rate debts on your Debt Hit List—will be sent to the top creditor on your Debt Hit List. Here's where you get to see all of your hard work in action. It's exciting to see the amount of money left after paying for your Needs grow bigger as you learn to cut back on your spending. Obviously you can't calculate how much money you'll have after covering your Needs until after you've paid all of those bills.

CONFIRM DEPOSIT

It should go without saying, but since you're writing out your checks in preparation for payday, confirm that your paycheck has successfully been direct deposited/cleared with the bank before you actually put the payments in the mail.

SPEND ON NEEDS ONLY

Writing out your payments completes one Spending Fast cycle and begins a new one. Continue to spend on Needs Only and find ways to reduce those Needs even more. As you are keeping track of your debits and credits throughout the Spending Fast cycle in your paper register, you will be able to keep tabs on how well you are—or are not—doing and can modify your behavior and spending to positively impact the end of cycle savings.

Now that you have an up-to-date, double-checked, accurate bank account balance, go ahead and pay all of your bills, following these steps:

For Your Very First Spending Fast Cycle

1. **Based on your Needs list, address the bills that are due.** Start writing checks for your Needs bills: rent or mortgage, utilities, cell phone, and other services. Be sure to carefully deduct each amount in your register as you write each check.

2. **Get out your Debt Hit List.** Pay the *minimum* amount due for all of your debts, *even for the top of your Debt Hit List.* (In subsequent Spending Fast cycles the amount paid to the top debt will be addressed in a different way. Paying the minimum for the top debt applies only to the first Spending Fast cycle.) Again, keep updating your bank account's balance in your register as you write a check for each bill.

   Since you carefully calculated your balance as you paid each bill, you should now have an accurate bank balance in your register (even if it does reflect a negative number). The next day when you confirm that your paycheck has successfully posted to your account, add that amount to your check register and update your balance. You should no longer be "in the red."

For Subsequent Spending Fast Cycles

Use this method if you know exactly how much you will be getting paid the following day:

1. **Zero out your account.** This may feel backward, but it's not. Since you've been spending on Needs Only (and as little as possible on those Needs) for your last Spending Fast cycle, and since you've been carefully

tracking each transaction in your account, you should have an accurate balance in your register. This entire amount—every single penny that's left in your register—is going to be sent to the top debt on your Debt Hit List. This is the exciting part because this is where you get to see how much your hard work the previous month has paid off. Also, please note that this is the one time it's okay to have a bank balance of zero, because you'll be paid the very next day.

2. **Based on your Needs list, address the bills that are due.** You will now be starting your next Spending Fast cycle with a clean slate and zero balance. Start writing checks for the bills on your Needs List: rent or mortgage, utilities, cell phone, cable, and other services. Be sure to carefully deduct each amount in your register as you write each check. Since you have zeroed out your account with your payment to the top debt on your Debt Hit List, your account will reflect a negative balance with each entry into your paper registry.

3. **Get out your Debt Hit List.** Pay the *minimum* amount due for all of the remaining debts. Again, keep updating your bank account balance in your register as you write a check for each debt. The next day, when you confirm that your paycheck has successfully posted to your account (and that it is indeed enough to cover the checks you've written out), add that amount to your check register and update your balance.

Use this method if you DO NOT know exactly how much you will be getting paid the following day:

1. **Based on your Needs list, address the bills that are due.** Start writing checks for the bills on your Needs list: rent or mortgage, utilities, cell phone, cable, and other services. Be sure to carefully deduct each amount in your register as you write each check.

2. **Get out your Debt Hit List.** Pay the *minimum* amount due for all of your debts except for the one at the top of your list. Keep updating your bank account's balance in your register as you write a check for each bill.

   Once you are left with the top debt on your Debt Hit List, stop. Since you carefully calculated your balance as you paid each bill, you should now have an accurate bank balance in your register (even if it does reflect a negative number). Once you find out what your paycheck amount is, enter that amount into the register, then recalculate your balance.

3. **Write the check for your top debt.** At this point you've written out your Needs bills and the minimum payments for all the debts on you Debt Hit List excluding the top debt on the list. Since you have an unpredictable income it's obviously important that you have enough money to pay for food, gas, and other daily expenses. Based on your Reverse Budget, calculate how much money you will likely need to survive until your next paycheck. Mentally deduct that amount from your paycheck and send the remaining amount to the top debt on your Debt Hit List. As you continue with your Spending Fast, money will accumulate and additional payments can be sent to the top debt on subsequent Spending Fast cycles.

Pat Yourself on the Back

I remember how amazing it felt to watch my payouts grow each month, while the balance on my number one debt withered away. It's a big deal, and you should be proud. It's likely that you'll be so excited by your diminishing debt that you'll find yourself happily (or almost happily) saying no to even more spending, and you'll find better ways to cut back on the cost of items on your Needs List. Well done.

The Master Savings Sheet: Watch Your Saving Skills Grow

It's important to focus on the positive, and that's why I highly recommend you create a Master Savings Sheet to track how much you're saving every month. It is an amazing feeling to end a Spending Fast cycle with a chunk of money (be it small or large) to send to your number one debt. I like to compete with myself, and this is a fun way to do that. I created a simple document that tracked how much money I had left after paying for all my Needs bills, so that I could congratulate myself each month as I was entering an even bigger number. The Master Savings Sheet is an important tool, because it's black-and-white, tangible proof that you're saving money, and making *tons* of progress! It may take a while to get those vile debts paid off, but the Master Savings Sheet provides immediate proof of your debt-reduction evolution, so track your progress as you go.

Let's Do This!

- ❑ Create your Debt Hit List. Highest-interest-rate (and emotionally heavy) debts are placed at the top.
- ❑ Obtain a paper check register.
- ❑ Track every addition and deduction in your register, double-checking online for accuracy and to be sure nothing was missed.
- ❑ Determine your Spending Fast cycle length.
- ❑ Work through the Payback Plan.
- ❑ List every payment on your Master Savings Sheet. Recalculate as you go so you maintain an accurate representation of the debts you owe and how much progress you have made!

END THE VICIOUS CYCLE OF ADMIRE, ACQUIRE, FEEL LIKE CRAP.

CHAPTER 7

Mastering Needs-Only Spending

Getting out of debt would be a lot easier if everyone could live in a rent-free bubble and survive without eating. Without having to pay for Needs like shelter and food, people would have a lot more money to put toward debt. But obviously, this isn't going to happen. You have Needs! And you just spent some meaningful time thinking about what those Needs really are. You're no longer going to thoughtlessly drop $20 on a bottle of expensive olive oil (during the Fast, at least) or pick up a pair of shoes "'cause they're on sale." You've started down the road to financial freedom, and mastering Needs-Only spending is what's going to get you there. Next I'm going to talk about how to stay committed to the Needs you have. It's time to start thinking about items on the Needs side of the list as you would about the fruits and veggies you need to eat to stay healthy. You know that broccoli and blueberries are better choices than the three-layer cake that calls out to you from the display case. When you make the right choices, you're operating as the best version of yourself, and making good choices builds confidence.

No More Woe

I know I just compared Needs-Only spending to eating fruits and vegetables. My point is that while you have to make sacrifices to getting yourself out of debt, it's so worth it in the end. What's not going to help you is feeling sorry for yourself. You can't think about what you're missing out on every time you walk past your favorite clothing store with a big SALE! sign in the window (you don't need another slimming blazer. Really). The Spending Fast is not about being miserable and feeling sorry for yourself; it's about revamping your relationship with money so that you can reach your goal of being debt-free. You'll be happy with all of the choices you've made the day you pull a credit card statement out of your mailbox and the balance reads zero. That day *will* come. Until then, you're going to have to enjoy the unexpected and sometimes subtle benefits that come along with Needs-Only spending.

You Are Not Defined by a Pair of Jeans or an iPhone

Once I got into the heart of the Spending Fast, I started to see how my spending habits were keeping me from living in reality. I spent too much time idolizing objects other people had. I used to really like doing yoga after work. Instead of focusing on the practice of yoga—breathing, stretching my body, quieting my mind—I was fixated on all the stuff other people had. I was zeroing in on the beautiful yoga pants with the contrasting colorful seams and the super-flattering tops with strappy backs. I even noted yoga mats, yoga towels, and water bottles—I wanted *everything*. Later, I would stalk my prey on Amazon, wasting hours of my life deciding what I should buy. As if an appropriately absorbant yoga towel would make me a better, more interesting person. So instead of coming home feeling relaxed and happy about my workout, I entered the vicious cycle of admire, acquire, feel like crap. Now when I go to yoga, I'm focused, and I actually enjoy the benefits.

Obviously I'm not saying yoga is the key to surviving the Spending Fast. My point is that it was a surprising realization to me that my autopilot spending habits were even ruining yoga! Once you're engaged in Needs-Only spending, you'll start to see life in a new way when you're not concentrating so heavily on what you want to buy next. I know it's exciting to get the newest iPhone or a cozy cardigan, but make a point to pay attention to the other great stuff in life: a successful project at work, a conversation with a good friend, or the feel of a long run in the morning. There are so many other parts of life to be enjoyed! I promise that a major sale at your favorite store will seem pointless once you start embracing the benefits of Needs-Only spending. Until then, try to keep the following positive thoughts in mind when you're having a rough time sticking to Needs-Only spending. Tell yourself:

> If I can get through this moment, the urge to spend will pass.
> Feeling sorry for myself will not erase my debt more quickly.
> I've taken a really big step in the right direction and am headed toward a zero balance on my credit card statement. Not only *can* I do this—I *am* doing this!
> I'm not the only one in this position. I've made the choice to get out of debt, and I'm getting there.

Changing Habits

If I'm going to be completely honest, one of the reasons the transition to Needs-Only spending is so hard is that it showcases some really regrettable spending habits. When I did the Spending Fast I was immediately confronted with some of the ridiculous ways I handled money, and I didn't like seeing myself in that light. I had to make some major changes in order to put myself in a better position to succeed. I realized pretty quickly that I had to rethink how I spent a lot of my free time, including how I dealt with social events. There were some irresponsible banking habits that had to be addressed. I also had to work hard to stop comparing myself to other people. It was a lot of work, but again, committing to follow the Spending Fast made me a better, more engaged person. I'm not sure I would have learned how damaging some of these habits were if I hadn't done the Spending Fast. One of the more obvious changes took place at the mall.

The Saturday (Late) Morning Mall Ritual

My husband and I had a screwy Saturday morning mall habit. We didn't go to the mall with a specific need, such as buying a wedding present for a friend or replacing something that had broken. We regularly drove the 2.9 miles in Aaron's bright teal-green Subaru with the bashed-in passenger door. When we got to the mall, I'd pick up my usual—a large nonfat extra-hot vanilla latte that cost $4.85—and then I was ready.

We would drift from store to store looking for things we "needed." For Aaron, who's naturally good with money, this was not a problematic way to spend a Saturday. But me? I couldn't contain myself. I was simultaneously obsessed, out of control, and full of shame. I had to buy. Now it seems kind of silly, but it was a habit. I was always buying new clothes or accessories for every little occasion. If a friend was having a housewarming party at her new apartment, clearly I needed a new shirt to wear to the event. If we were meeting coworkers for happy hour appetizers at a rooftop bar downtown, then I had better get some new earrings. It didn't take much to convince me I should spend money. It could be an upcoming event that I had to buy something new for, or an item could simply catch my eye. If the words *Ohh . . . I like that* crossed my mind for even a split second, I was done. Sold. Another easy justifier to my overspending? For a long time I didn't have a washer and dryer. I masterfully told myself that if I had more clothes, I could stretch out the time between my painful once-a-month eleven-load laundry sessions even further. My quest to acquire thirty pairs of socks and thirty pairs of underwear didn't seem that strange to me. I felt like an ingenious problem solver.

My affinity for all things new was costing me plenty of money, and I didn't want cheap, disposable clothing or my hatred of the chore of washing laundry to be the reason I couldn't have (or even envision) a life without debt. When I put myself on the Spending Fast, I realized that I actually felt an obligation to buy something every time I went into a store. It felt weird leaving empty-handed. I had to adjust to this strange new feeling of not spending money and leaving without a bag in my hand. It became really clear that I was stockpiling all the items I thought I might need, rather than living my life and letting my real needs materialize on their own. I had to consciously remind myself that I wasn't a squirrel that needed to hoard a surplus of inventory for the upcoming winter.

I felt terrible about spending all that money, but I didn't know how to change my ways. The Spending Fast finally allowed me to focus on more than material objects and start aspiring to live autonomously.

When I understood that I didn't have to spend every day, I felt free instantly. My shoulders relaxed. Everything felt lighter. The mall trip was the clearest example I had of my "need to spend," and I was relieved to start creating more sensible (and less expensive) routines.

When I started the Spending Fast, going to the mall was obviously out. So was buying earrings expressly for rooftop gatherings. Better, more authentic activities replaced the ones that cost me money. I'm certainly not saying that having get-togethers with friends isn't important, but I learned that it's not something I needed to do practically every night just because I hadn't thought of other options. Aaron and I found some great stuff to do together that didn't involve drinking expensive coffee while wandering around the mall. I discovered that I love making coffee at home using a French press, which doesn't cost any more than a standard Mr. Coffee machine—and bonus, you don't have to buy filters for it. The coffee tasted a million times better, even if it was of the generic store-brand $1.50-a-half-pound variety. We also worked out together, usually running or lifting weights. I even dug out my snazzy Rollerblades and got exercise zipping around the park in them. Some mornings we did our grocery shopping together. If Aaron wanted to go to the mall, I realized I wasn't missing out if I stayed home. Before long, I didn't even miss wandering around the mall spending money on stuff I didn't need.

It can be uncomfortable to change rituals and routines, but if they're resulting in the loss of copious amounts of money, you have a good reason to shake things up.

If you're struggling to find new, healthy activities, consider the following ideas:

Appreciate where you are. You've started to make some great choices about your financial well-being and you are taking action to have a better future.

Relax and hobby it up. A lot of times when we spend *money* we're trying to fill some sort of void. Instead, spend *time* doing something you enjoy—such as reading, crafting, or drawing.

Take care of yourself. Get plenty of sleep, drink the recommended half gallon of water per day, and eat nutrient-rich foods.

Dive into big goals. I wanted to live a more authentic life, and running and working out fit in with that vision. If you want to be a writer, join a writer's group, or dedicate time each day to jot down thoughts or write a short story. Identify your big goals and start taking steps to achieve them.

Dabble with monthly themes. Dedicate one month to organization, one month to fitness, one month to artistic pursuits.

You Don't Know How They Paid for That: Stop Comparing Yourself to Other People

Trying to keep up with the neighbors is a big reason a lot of people are in debt. It's easy to think (especially thanks to glossy magazines and beautiful images on Pinterest) that a large, expertly decorated house and an expensive car are things we all *deserve*. I used to assume that people who had nice things that I coveted—like amazing furniture, beautiful clothes, and even giant sparkly diamonds—could afford them. But how on earth could I actually know that? No one knew that I was drowning in debt, so it's entirely possible Mr. and Mrs. Massive Diamond Ring didn't actually have a penny to their name.

Focus instead on what you do have and the choices you've made (hey, like that one to get out of debt) and keep working toward that autonomous, totally debt-free life. The next time you find yourself getting envious of someone's amazing outfit or super-plush couch, think about the following before you go on a credit card charging spree:

You have no idea if that person could actually afford the [*insert item causing envy here*].

Attractive things are not a cure-all. (At least not long term.)

If you get your shit together and pay off your debts you will eventually be able to afford to buy something you admire from time to time. And you'll be able to do it guilt-free.

Someone else's enviable jewelry, fancy vacation, or electronic device doesn't actually have the power to make you feel crappy. Only you do. So cut it out already. Focus on the good in your life, not what's lacking.

It's Okay to Be "Selfish" Sometimes (and the Spending Fast Is One of Those Times)

It can be really tough whacking your way through debt. You might have stopped going to restaurants or movies with your friends. Perhaps you've decided to skip your cousin's destination wedding, even though you've never been to Barcelona and you're dying to go. You've decided to put yourself and your financial health first, and that is a bold, empowering move to make. I found that there were times when what I needed to do to stick to my plan required some selfishness on my end. Aaron wasn't exactly excited when I imposed a $3 gift-giving limit on Valentine's Day. While I wanted to recognize my husband's desire to celebrate a romantic holiday, I wanted to be out of debt even more. Although focusing on Needs-Only spending by cutting down on the money you use to buy gifts for other people may seem selfish at first blush, it's anything but. I personally can't think of anything less selfish to do than forgoing a box of chocolates or a dinner out for a debt-free foundation that you can build a solid life on together.

It's really easy to feel guilted into spending money when it's going to make someone else happy. Telling others "I really can't" or giving an outright no isn't an easy undertaking, especially when it's not your MO. At times it's hard to do, but know that it's okay to put yourself first. A good friend is going to graciously get over the fact that you had to pass on attending her elaborate seven-course birthday dinner at the luxe restaurant. I started to see how putting other people's desires over my own perpetuated the mess I was in.

When I started working at a magazine in New York City, I was very conscious of the image I was projecting. I was making very little money at the time, but didn't want that to stop me from hanging out with all the industry people after work. We'd go out for expensive drinks and sometimes food, and all of this automatically went on my credit card. Before I knew it, I was $8,000 in debt. Now that I have more experience, I know I could have saved myself the debt. I had fun, but good colleagues like you for who you are, not because you are always available for after-work drinks.　　　　　　　　　　　　　—Caroline

It's hard to put yourself first, and declining an invitation isn't always just about the fear of missing out on an incredible party. There are so many deeply embedded reasons people have a hard time saying no. You need to get comfortable with the idea that you and your financial health must come first at this time in your life. If you're like me, you've probably encountered the following situations and have found yourself saying yes when you knew it wasn't in your best interest to do so. Just like most anything in life, saying no gets easier with practice.

You don't want to hurt anyone's feelings. I get it. Debt, though? We know that carrying that weight hurts more than missing a dinner or drinks.

You're known for your easygoing nature. Yep, me too. Focus on the grand prize at the end of all this (*a zero balance* on all your debt) and let that take priority over your agreeability.

You don't want things to be awkward. Wanna know what's more awkward than turning down invites? (This is tough love time, people.) Getting evicted, filing for bankruptcy, having to ask friends for a couple dollars because you haven't eaten in days, getting your car repossessed in the dead of night. Don't go there if you can avoid it. *Which you can.*

You're not into conflict. If one of your friends doesn't get why you're not available, tell him about your situation. Being afraid of the conflict is often worse than the conflict itself. Face it head on.

You don't want to miss out. It's easy to convince yourself you'll miss out on great opportunities (Networking! Experiences! The latest gossip!) if you don't go out and spend money like usual. The Spending Fast is all about opportunity—getting your life in order. Having your shit together, in my experience, is one giant door opener.

No More Bank Balance Surprises: Getting Organized

One time I sent a curt e-mail to a really nice guy who did some website design work for me. The reason for the e-mail: He hadn't immediately cashed a check I'd sent him. I didn't keep track of how much money I had in my account (apart from quick glances when I logged in online), so by the time he deposited his payment months later, I had only a few bucks left in my account. Not surprisingly, the check bounced and the overdraft fees started rolling in. Pacing my apartment and foaming at the mouth like a deranged (but lovable) Gary Busey, I blamed my website designer for causing my account to go into the red. I furiously typed out a wildly inappropriate e-mail that said something to the effect of "Are there any other checks you haven't cashed yet!?!?!?!?" Um. This error was totally not his fault—it was all mine. At the time I thought it was too boring to keep track of my money. I figured I had overdraft protection on my account, and it would suck to get the fees if I spent more than what was in my account, but in the grand scheme of things it wasn't *that* big of a deal. Might as well just add it to the pile of debt I already have! I thought being penalized with fees here and there wouldn't make that much of a difference.

I would routinely call up the bank and ask, yet again, to please have the overdraft fees waived. I didn't have the money to cover what I was buying with my debit card or the checks I was writing, but I was also racking up $25 fees like crazy, digging an even deeper hole for myself. I gave the bank a couple of sob stories, some real and some fabricated. My tales ranged from "My wallet got stolen" (it hadn't), "I'm going to head over and deposit money right away!" (I didn't have any to deposit), and "Gosh, I have no idea how I let that happen! It definitely won't happen again!" (it would). The bank did waive a few of the fees for me, but the customer service reps had heard it all before and were quickly over my stories of feigned sorrow. It was time to take control, get organized, and track *Every. Single. Penny.*

Keeping on top of my money finally helped me feel like I knew what was going on with my finances. I'm not going to lie, writing down every penny I spent was tedious—to the point where I would actually choose not to spend money so that I wouldn't have to log another debit into my register. I saved all my receipts in my purse, entered them all at the end of the day, then stuffed them into my trusty manila envelope. This task helped me stay intent on my purpose. I couldn't make the excuse of "Oh, I couldn't include that purchase because I was rushed and in the middle of a crowded store at the time." If I committed to writing down my expenses at the end of the day, I stuck to the plan, because it was easier than trying to do everything on the spot. If I missed a night of inputting purchases into my check register, then I did it the next day. Recording my expenses showed me that I liked being current with my money. I was encouraged by the progress I was making even if it was just as simple as maintaining the new habit of writing my purchases and income in my paper register. I was able to carefully weigh buying decisions because I knew how much money was in my account at any time. It didn't matter if a check I'd written took a while to clear, because I'd taken the time to deduct the check's amount from the balance when I wrote it out (as I should have been doing all along)—and so the money for that check would be in my account until the check was processed. Knowing my balance also helped me stick to my Needs-Only spending. If I was at the grocery store and knew my balance was getting low, I would think twice about buying butter that wasn't on sale or the grated (and more expensive) cheese.

It may seem like a pain, but setting up a system for keeping track of your money is a really important part of getting your financial act together. Here are just a few things to think about while sorting out a tracking technique that works for you:

Keep everything in one place. Receipts, bills, and bank statements should have a specific, easily accessible spot. If you access your statements electronically, download a copy to a folder on your computer.

Designate a specific time to deal with your transactions. I needed to know exactly how much I had at all times, and I didn't want to get behind, so I logged mine nightly. Get into a routine and stick to it.

Don't forget to include automatic debits (if you haven't turned them off yet) and checks you've written.

Sign up for low-balance alerts. Your bank probably has an account feature that sends you a text message if your balance falls below a certain level. Just remember that this alert isn't a replacement for your actually knowing how much money you have. It should serve only as a safeguard to help you discover if you've made a mistake tracking your account balance.

Think About What You *Can* Spend Money On

I'll be totally honest—there were many times I wanted to give up on the Spending Fast. It got especially trying around the third month. Frankly, I was bored. I hadn't yet fully embraced my newfound, uncomplicated, and modest lifestyle, and I missed buying stuff. I hadn't really figured out a way to hang out with my friends that didn't involve spending money, and Aaron was sick of me mooching off him. He was getting good at being able to tell if I was going to say, "Hey, you gonna eat that?" or "Can I have a sip?" He'd beat me to the punch with an expert-level side-eye, stopping me midsentence. I was tired of wearing black all the time—my boss at the time even asked me if my black wardrobe was a "Johnny Cash thing." Nah, just a frugal thing. I was completely out of my really good coffee, and I was buying the least expensive off-brand grounds I could find.

While drinking bad coffee sucked, the worst part of the Spending Fast up to that point was turning down an invitation to go on a trip with my husband. I was saying no to a lot of invites at the time, but this one hit me hard. Aaron was taking a trip to Portland, Oregon, to visit his brother, Matthew. I envisioned them drinking coffee so good that in years to come, it would be referenced in stories: "Remember that time when we had the most amazing coffee in the world?" And surely they'd hike through forests of the tallest, lushest, greenest trees, while exotic, never-seen-before birds serenaded them with magical songs. They'd stop to enjoy a perfectly packed picnic lunch while lounging on a red-and-white gingham blanket, and a rainbow would hover so vibrantly above them that if they were to reach out, they'd be left with a dusting of color on their fingertips. Approximately 5,478 inside jokes would be created during this magical lunch in the forest, and I'd spend the rest of my life being told, "You know, you *just* had to be there."

The novelty of the Spending Fast had worn off and reality had sunk in. Aaron was tired of my "experiment" and my decision to do the Spending Fast without his prior "approval." Needless to say, the Spending Fast was wearing out its welcome. I started to think things like, *Hey! I did the Spending Fast for three solid months! That's pretty good. This is so intense, no one would think less of me if I didn't make it for the entire year, right?*

I needed to take a step back and reflect on the progress I had made:

In just three months my deep-seated thoughts about money were already morphing.

I was able to pay off a large amount of debt in that short time. What would happen if I kept going?

I had felt like such a loser for not being able to control my spending, and that was changing. Now I felt positive.

Taking the time to look back on how I'd changed my habits showed me that I was stronger than I ever knew I was, and my decision to do the Spending Fast was reaffirmed every time I sent a sizable payment to my creditors. I realized I had to have stamina if I wanted to reach my goal of one year. Around this time I started getting comments from readers of my blog. People were rooting for me and letting me know that I had inspired them to think about their own money in a new way. I had nine months to go, and I wanted to succeed. It was at that point that I made a decision to stop thinking about all the stuff I couldn't buy and to focus on what I *could* buy. Focusing on what I was allowed to buy, all the stuff on my Needs list, sometimes gave me the strength to make it just one more day without looking longingly over at the Wants side.

Whenever I was at a low point, I folded my Wants and Needs List down the middle and looked at just the Needs side. It may sound strange, but I'd say to myself, *I can buy groceries! I can dye my hair whenever I want! I can put together my photography exhibits!* Perhaps less thrilling, but equally important, I also recognized that I could pay my rent, utilities, gas, medical copays, and so on without struggling. Realizing I was able to pay for all the stuff on the Needs side, stress-free, was invigorating. It was yet another marker of my progression from Spender to Saver. And more importantly, every day that I endured the fight of me vs. my debt, I was defending my new way of life, ensuring that I'd never allow my finances to get that messy again. I constantly told myself that I had to bust out of my money comfort zone. Fundamentally, I knew that changing meant doing things differently. I savored those trips to the grocery store, and I encourage you to do the same. You're putting yourself in a position to pay the bills without anxiety. That's something to celebrate.

Needs-Only Spending, Upgraded

I've spent a lot of time talking about Needs-Only spending. It's great to go to a store and buy stuff you need and leave with no buyer's remorse whatsoever. At this point in the Spending Fast I really started to see how sticking to Needs-Only spending was making a big impact on my debt. Rather than let myself get tempted to loosen the purse strings, I decided to deepen my commitment to Needs-Only spending. I started to think about how I could cover all my Needs and have even more money left to send to creditors each month. The trickiest areas tended to be groceries and clothing. While I wasn't buying any new clothes during my year of the Spending Fast, that didn't mean they didn't still try to lure me with their siren song. I constantly worked really hard to find ways to cut back.

Groceries: Shop Like Your Mother

If your mom is anything like mine, she probably gave you a classic piece of advice about grocery shopping: "Don't go shopping while you're hungry." This seems fairly obvious, yet until the Spending Fast it was advice I chose to ignore. Realizing that groceries were one of the few precious Needs-Only items I allowed myself to spend money on, I wanted to stretch every penny and shop as smartly as possible. I realized I should listen to my mom's advice, as well as figure out a few other ways to spend less at the grocery store. See if you can make some of the following tips work for you too.

> **Do the "fake out."** Buy your name-brand coffee, cereal, etc. the first time. Save the name-brand container, then buy the generic version of the item when you run out. Fill the used name-brand container with the generic version of the item. Continue refilling the container with the off-brand version.

Embrace oatmeal. It's healthy and filling, you can make it a million different ways, and oh yeah, it's dirt cheap. Buying whole-grain, old-fashioned oats in bulk is an especially good idea.

Buy special ingredients at ethnic markets. They will likely be significantly less expensive than at your local grocery store.

Pick food that can last a long time or that freezes well to avoid Empty Pantry Syndrome.* Foods that keep on going include nuts, rice, flour, peanut butter, oats, beans, noodles. Canned goods can obviously stick around a long time. You can make a number of dishes using cans or pouches of tuna. Use flour to get creative with pancake, waffle, and crepe recipes.

Consider becoming a "secret shopper" to get paid while receiving free groceries.

Rebrand leftovers as "déjà vu meals." If you have to, feign happiness about having your favorite meal multiple times. "You again! So good to see you!"

Perfect a few go-to recipes. Keep them simple and delicious. Freeze or package leftovers in single-serve containers for the next day's lunch. Again, this helps fight Empty Pantry Syndrome, as well as I Was Running Late So I Couldn't Pack My Lunch disease.

Get your cheap snacks and cereals at the local dollar store. This is only advisable, though, if the dollar store isn't a spending trigger for you.

Avoid recipes that call for unusual ingredients, unless you're absolutely sure you'll use them several times. They're not worth spending the extra money. (If you do find yourself with a bunch of special ingredients that you have no idea what to do with, look around on Epicurious.com for inspiration.)

---

* *Empty Pantry Syndrome occurs when you have no staples on hand and have no ideas about what to make for dinner, so you call your closest take-out joint.*

Resist the temptation to stock up on supplies as if you won't be leaving the house for two years. There's a difference between having staples on hand and preparing for a zombie apocalypse.

Ask for grocery store gift cards for birthdays and holidays.

Shop locally and in season. You know how every frugally minded food blogger will tell you to shop locally and in season? And to avoid processed and packaged food? That's because it's really good advice—eating this way is better for your health and your wallet.

Um, But I Like Super-Expensive Organic Food

There's no doubt that it's preferable to buy food that's not full of chemicals and pesticides. Many people worry that they'll have to forgo healthy food choices when doing the Spending Fast, because organic produce and dairy products, cage-free eggs, and free-range chicken tend to cost quite a bit more than their humble counterparts. We've touched on this nuance before; you don't necessarily have to throw your values out the windows in order to cut back on your food costs. You simply need to redefine some of your priorities and get creative about how you do your food shopping.

Reprioritize: Does That Kiwi Really Need to Be Organic?

While it's nice to be surrounded by wholesome, organic produce, not every single thing you put in your cart has to be organic (at least not for health reasons). If you haven't heard of the Dirty Dozen or the Clean Fifteen, let me introduce you. In this case, the Dirty Dozen are not convicted murderers (film buffs will know what I'm referring to), but rather are produce determined by the Environmental Working Group's Pesticides in Produce report to contain the highest levels of pesticide residues. If you want to cut back on your grocery costs, buy organic versions of only the following fruits and veggies:

Apples

Celery

Cherry tomatoes

Cucumbers

Grapes

Nectarines (imported)

Peaches

Potatoes

Snap peas (imported)

Spinach

Strawberries

Sweet bell peppers

It should be noted that within the past couple years, two more veggies have been added to the list. Leafy greens such as kale and collards and hot peppers are now also officially considered "dirty."

The Clean Fifteen, as you may have guessed, refers to foods that are not as high in pesticides or that have inedible peels that limit your exposure to pesticides. You can buy the cheaper, conventional versions of:

Asparagus

Avocados

Cabbage

Cantaloupe

Cauliflower

Eggplant

Grapefruit

Kiwi

Mangoes

Onions

Papayas

Pineapple

Sweet corn

Sweet peas (frozen)

Sweet potatoes

Find a Food Co-Op Near You

If organic foods are a major expense for you, consider joining a food co-op, a member-owned grocery store. Co-ops generally offer all of their products at a specific percentage above wholesale cost, which will save you a ton of money. Co-ops work in different ways; some charge a fee to be a member. The Park Slope Food Co-op in Brooklyn, New York, the mother of all food co-ops, requires all members to work a monthly shift in the store in addition to paying a small investment when they join. Since labor is one of the biggest costs of running a business, a major savings is passed on to members by having them share staff duties. Check out food co-ops in your area and see what they offer.

Buy a CSA Share

CSA stands for community sponsored agriculture, in which a farm or farms will offer shares to the general public. It's kind of like buying a subscription to a farmer's produce. Usually in return for paying for your share, you'll receive a box of produce (or maybe dairy products and eggs, depending on the farm you pick) on a weekly basis. Some CSA programs require that you pick up your food from the farm itself or a packaging center, and others deliver right to your front door. The cool thing about having a CSA share is that not only do you get extra fresh, seasonal food, but you also help out a local farmer.

Taming the Biggest Temptation of All: Clothes

It's really easy to be lured by the call of crisp, new clothes. I know a lot of people who put "clothes" on the Wants side of their lists because when it came down to it, they had to admit they had a lot of clothes, and that it would be entirely possible to make do with what they already owned. Once you're in the midst of your Spending Fast, not listing clothes as a Need may start to feel totally insane. What was I thinking? *Winter is coming. I need new pants, sweaters, scarves—everything.*

I get it. Clothes really do seem like a Need (because technically, you're required to wear them). I was really proud that I made it through the Spending Fast without buying new clothes. Here's how I did it:

Purposefully Limit Your Choices

Black. Stick with black clothing and shoes. It's flattering and forgiving, and basic black works for anyone. You can easily redye or touch up a piece of black clothing if its color fades—I did this often, including occasionally fixing scuff marks on shoes using a permanent black marker. A great feature of black clothing is that it's difficult to determine the price of the piece. A $7 black T-shirt is barely distinguishable from one that cost $50. Black is almost always appropriate in the workplace, and you can pull off black during the day or at night. It's basic enough that you could wear the same pair of black pants every day with a different top and no one would even notice. I did this all the time, washing the pants as they needed it.

If the idea of all black bores you, make black and white your signature, or create a capsule wardrobe for more variety. A capsule wardrobe is made up of thirty-three items—tops, bottoms, outerwear, and accessories—from which you create all your outfits. TheProject333.com is a great resource if you want detailed information on how to create your own capsule wardrobe. A perk of limiting your choices about what to wear each day is that you'll have one less decision to make each morning. Tim Ferriss, author of *The 4-Hour Workweek*, is a big advocate against *decision fatigue*. Decision fatigue, no joke, is a condition in which you actually become less productive because you're so mentally exhausted from making decisions. President Barack Obama has even said that he's trying to cut back on decision making, that he doesn't want to think about what he's eating or wearing. That makes sense. Why waste energy on choosing a tie when you have to make choices that impact the fate of the world? President Obama isn't the only one who doesn't want to be bothered with wardrobe decisions. Other well-known adopters of the monotone "uniform" wardrobe style include Vera Wang, Hetty Green, Mark Zuckerberg, Steve Jobs, Karl Lagerfeld, Donna Karan, and Albert Einstein.

Accessories Are Your Friends

Instead of spending your hard-earned money on tops, bottoms, and shoes, focus on accessories. They're less expensive than other wardrobe pieces, and they can quickly and dramatically change the entire look of an outfit. Necklaces and scarves work well for women. For guys, cool ties and playful socks can make a big difference.

Trends, Trends, Trends

I'm just gonna say it. Don't follow clothes that are trending. On an impulse, I bought a pair of tan booties with fringe on the side. They were super-cute and I loved them when I purchased them. They have not, however, stood the test of time. The next year, there was no fringe on anyone's boots, and wouldn't you know it, I found myself charmed by a pair of tan booties with *no* fringe. Classic and timeless wins out every time in the style department, especially when you're trying to save money.

I'll add that, while on the Spending Fast, it's a good idea to stay away from fashion blogs and magazines. They basically exist to make you desperately want trendy pieces, and it's easy to end up feeling inferior because of all the clothes you can't buy. Fashion blogs and magazines can be a major trigger for shame-induced spending. Unless you know you can resist, it's best to avoid looking at these types of social media.

For fashion inspiration on the cheap, here are some of my favorite frugal fashion and style blogs:

BudgetBlonde.com
CheapChicas.com
FrugalBeautiful.com
PennyChic.com
PSIMadeThis.com
RavingFashionista.com
refinery29.com
SHEfinds.com

No More So-Sos

Go through all your clothes and accessories and only keep the items that you feel absolutely amazing in (bonus—you can make *money* from selling all those items you no longer want—we'll talk about how to do this later). Marie Kondo, author of *The Life-Changing Magic of Tiding Up: The Japanese Art of Decluttering and Organizing,* has an extremely effective technique. She says you should discard anything you own that does not "spark joy"—that is, after you thank the objects slated for the heave-ho for their service. It might seem counterproductive (and scary) to purge your closet of clothes you don't wear when you know you're not going to be buying new clothes in the near future—but stick with me on this. By getting rid of all the subpar, mediocre pieces that you feel only so-so in, you'll be left with the items you love. I'd rather have five pieces of clothing I'm completely crazy about than twenty-five pieces I'm ambivalent about. What's left in your closet will feel like a brand-new wardrobe that was created especially for you, because in a way it was! Since going forward you'll feel amazing in what you're wearing, the desire for new clothes will lessen and you'll be happy with what you have because you'll be feeling (and looking) super-hot. You'll have more time on your hands too, since you won't have as many clothes to wash and put away.

A clean, streamlined wardrobe also means that getting ready in the mornings will be a lot easier. Instead of searching through piles of shoddy sweaters for your all-time favorite top, it will be neatly hanging in your closet ready to be matched up with one of your three pairs of incredible, derriere-enhancing pants.

DON'T BUY THE WARDROBE ITEM . . .

If you can't sit down in it.

If it doesn't fit.

If it would look great if it was tailored but you've never taken anything to the tailor, ever.

If it doesn't look good from every angle.

If you want it only because it's inexpensive or because it's on super-mega sale.

If you're texting pictures to your friends from the dressing room because you can't decide how you feel about it. (That's a major red flag, by the way. I'll be willing to bet that you're trying to convince yourself that you like the item even though you know deep down that you don't really dig it.)

If you're sure you'll be able to figure out what to wear the item with but you can't quickly come up with an idea of how to do so.

Just because someone on the Internet told you it was cute.

If you don't love it enough to throw out one of your current pieces in exchange.

If you're buying it because you like the idea of it more than the reality of it. (Buying on theory gets expensive!)

If you just want to be the type of person who would wear an item like this.

If you're buying it for a future event that you're not sure will ever happen.

If you don't feel compelled to wear it out of the store right that minute or to work the very next morning.

If you have to learn a skill to make the piece work (like how to walk in wobbly five-inch heels).

Just because you feel obligated to make a purchase.

SHOULD I BUY IT?

$ $ $ $ $

DO I NEED IT?

NO ← / → YES → DO YOU ALREADY OWN SOMETHING LIKE IT?

ALL RIGHT. THAT WAS QUICK. YOU HAVE YOUR ANSWER. NO MONEY SPENT.
↳ HECK YEAH!

MAYBE
I COULD DEFINITELY CONVINCE MYSELF THAT I NEED IT! I DO WORK HARD AFTERALL!
↳ C'MON NOW. NO MORE WINDOW SHOPPING. GO ON HOME.

YES ↙

YOU DON'T NEED ANOTHER ONE. USE UP THE OLD ONE. WEAR IT OUT. TRUST ME

THIS IS OKAY! GOOD, ACTUALLY!

NO ↓

WELL, NOW THIS IS INTEREST-ING! NOW ASK YOURSELF: "IS IT WELL MADE?" "WILL IT LAST ME A LONG TIME?" "IS IT A CLASSIC STYLE THAT I WON'T GET SICK OF?" "DO I EVEN LIKE IT?" "WILL IT GO WITH WHAT I ALREADY OWN?" DO YOU WANT TO SPEND THE TIME TO MAINTAIN IT? "DOES THIS PURCHASE SUPPORT MY LONG TERM GOALS?" DO YOU LOVE IT? DO YOU??!

YES TO ALL?
↓
GO HOME & SLEEP ON IT.

SLEEP WELL? GOOD, CUZ IT'S BACK TO BUSINESS.

NOW, YOU DON'T HAVE TO SPEND ANY $. TODAY IS A GOOD DAY TO CHANGE YOUR LIFE. STILL WANT TO BUY IT?

↓ YES.↗ DO YOU HAVE ANY DEBT? ANY AT ALL?

NOPE! ↙
WELL, LOOK AT YOUR FINE SELF! YOU'VE PAID OFF YOUR DEBT & HAVE REALLY THOUGHT THIS THROUGH! MAKE YOUR WAY TO THE REGISTER! IT'S TRUE!

NOW, ASK YOURSELF, IS IT EXPENSE WORTHY? DO YOU WANT TO SPEND ALL THAT TIME AT WORK TO PAY FOR THIS? IS IT OVERPRICED? CAN YOU FIND IT ELSEWHERE CHEAPER? HUH??! HUH???!!?

↓ NO? THAT'S A-OKAY BECAUSE...

NO. GOOD DECISION!

→ YES. SORRY. THE BUCK STOPS HERE. IT'S A NO-GO.

YES TO ALL THE Q'S ↓

NO THAT'S THAT. THE END.

BUT! LOOK AT YOU SAVING!
↳ OH YEAH!
MONEY IN THE BANK!

$ $ $ $ $ $ $

$ Let's Do This!

❑ Focus on what you *can* spend money on: Needs Only. Fold your Wants and Needs List in half and look only at the Needs side.

❑ Preplan for how you will handle situations where you feel pressured to spend money with or on family or friends.

❑ Reflect on the amazing progress you've made so far. You're learning how to take the focus off things and tell yourself no. That's huge.

❑ Keep focused on your mission: *No debt.*

CHAPTER 8

Attack the Debt, Adjust to Your New Life, and Take It a Step Further

Money touches every area of our lives. People like to say that money doesn't matter and money isn't the most important thing, but we all know that your relationship with money has a huge impact on the quality of your life. When my finances were spiraling out of control, I was demoralized, guilty, and ashamed. How did I get myself into such a mess? Why couldn't I control my spending? I couldn't even get my debt reined in by using nonextreme measures that worked for other people. I had to go way beyond a budget to a straight-up Spending Fast to see any progress at all. My money problems made me feel like crap, and yet I believed spending *more* would make me feel better. But that feeling didn't last long. I could shop, spend, and push my money problems aside for a while—but the debt was still there at the end of the day.

Taking care of this hideous problem by doing the Spending Fast brought instant relief. Knowing I was taking measures to deal with my debt made me feel empowered, energized, and proactive. I was really happy about the positive steps the Spending Fast helped me take. However, I needed to be sure that I kept at it and didn't fall off the Spending Fast wagon. As I progressed with the Fast, I made some even bigger changes that helped me keep moving forward and attack the debt head on.

I wish I could say that once I finished my Wants and Needs List I was 100 percent on track with the Spending Fast and didn't spend any more money. Remember my last binge? That list of last-minute, pre–Spending Fast purchases was a real indication of how out of control my spending was, and how careful I would need to be about sticking to my plan. In my head, I was picking up a few "essentials" before going completely Wants-free. None of those items turned out to be the slightest bit helpful. The purchases were impulsive and frivolous. I told you earlier that one of my last pre–Spending Fast purchases was dry shampoo—I mean, it's not that hard to wash your hair with *real shampoo*. I had a lot to learn about what was a necessity and what wasn't. Likewise, rubber stamps, another pre-Fast purchase, weren't going to help me get through the Spending Fast, but a commitment to take action would. That binge just proved, again, that I needed to stick to the Spending Fast if I was ever going to be debt-free.

Don't Be Afraid to Share

It's not unusual to be ashamed of debt, but secrets aren't good for anyone. As you know, I decided to go public about my situation—I was wide open about the fact that I was having financial troubles. I was getting more excited about the Spending Fast and realized that sharing my experience with friends and family was helping me stay focused and would increase my likelihood of succeeding. My twin sister, Kelly, was really curious about the Spending Fast and had tons of questions about how I was going to manage without spending money on anything but my Needs. *What are you going to do about Christmas? Are there going to be presents? How are you going to get clothes for work? Are you ever going to splurge at the grocery store and buy nice chocolate or a pint of Ben & Jerry's? You need groceries, right??? Chocolate is a grocery. Does that mean it's okay?* At the time, I didn't necessarily have answers to all of her questions; I still had a lot to think through. I just knew that I had to at least make this attempt at getting out of debt.

I decided to start a blog about my experience three days before I started the Fast.

I was hoping that by publicly detailing my experience, I'd be keeping myself in check. If I was writing about the Spending Fast, it would make me think twice about buying winter coats and art from Etsy. I had decided that if I "messed up I was gonna fess up," so I thought long and hard about making purchases. I didn't want to have to admit to my mistakes publicly on the blog.

By the way, I'm not saying you need to start a blog or make a public announcement about your Spending Fast. However, continuing to share your commitment to living a debt-free life by spending money only on Needs with the people closest to you is an important part of the plan.

It's entirely possible that at this point in the Fast you'll need the support of the people you've told. I knew there would come a time when I wanted to quit, but since I had told so many people about what I was doing, I kept going. I also found that I had people unofficially checking in on me. It was really nice to know that my friends and family were supportive and interested in helping me reach my goal of being debt-free. Because I was constantly updating people on my progress, they could see that I was serious. It was very empowering to show people that I could follow through on such a difficult challenge.

On the flip side, it was great to be able to share the news when I had a major success. It was fun to announce that I'd had a month where I'd paid off more debt than I ever had before, or when I managed to knock a credit card account off my Debt Hit List. I also continued to use the Spending Fast as my "bad guy" if anyone was giving me a hard time about not taking part in something that cost money. I'd pull the "I would love to hang out with you, but you know, I'm doing the Spending Fast" card. I'd add a massive eye roll, acting like it was a complete drag, as if I couldn't join my friend because my super-strict parents wouldn't let me go out that night. In reality, I was relieved to have an easy out. I was like the kid who secretly loves doing homework—sticking to my Spending Fast commitment was thrilling. If your first foray into Needs-Only spending has left you feeling blue, anxious, lonely, or overwhelmed, seriously consider reaching out to your support team. You deserve a round of applause for everything you've accomplished so far.

Buckets of Time: How Are You Going to Fill Them?

As the Spending Fast progressed I was happily getting mega amounts of debt paid off, but there were other, unexpected nonmonetary developments happening too. My quality of life was changing in subtle but important ways. Where just a short time ago I was all about the hunt and thrill of object acquisition, I now had something I didn't have before: *time*. Lots and lots of time. At first it was strange, and I didn't always know what to do with myself now that I wasn't constantly busy with superficial things, such as collecting cake stands and going out to new places for brunch every weekend. Busyness is glorified in American culture, and it initially felt wrong to suddenly have time to spare. I also had to face the fact that scrolling through the Anthropologie website in search of the perfect shower curtain didn't leave me feeling all soft and fuzzy about myself at the end of the day. I thought my old spending habits had taken away only my money, but in reality, they had also taken a toll on how I felt about myself. On the upside, I now had time to do something about that.

At the start of the Fast, I wanted to shift my priorities and become less self-focused, less self-involved. In my midtwenties I volunteered at a SafeHouse, a women's shelter for victims of domestic violence, on a crisis line. I went through the training, studied the cycle of abuse, and learned the questions to ask during a call and how to respond to what callers were saying. When a bed opened up at the shelter, I talked women through what documents to gather in preparation for fleeing their situation. When women and children arrived at the door, it was satisfying to know they were out of harm's way; being part of the mission to protect them felt fulfilling. Soon after I stopped working at the shelter I increased my spending. When I wasn't helping others, I ended up with an emptiness that I filled with shopping. I'd made the mistake of thinking I could feel good about myself by having my life *look* perfect, with coordinating plates and embroidered tea towels, when in reality, I needed to take some sort of meaningful action to settle my restlessness. I had to spend my time in a worthwhile way and get outside of myself again.

As the Spending Fast went on, I noticed that I was able to direct my thoughts toward others in a way I hadn't been able to do when spending money was the answer to every dilemma I was faced with. Recently, a friend of mine lost a parent. Pre–Spending Fast, I would have thought about what I could buy to let her know I was there for her—flowers and a card? Instead, even though I was nervous I'd say the wrong thing, I picked up the phone. She sounded genuinely happy that I had reached out. I could have written "I'm here for you" in a card, but that wouldn't have held the same weight as connecting with someone in a direct and personal way.

It may feel really weird to have time open up. It's important to embrace this challenge and find something meaningful to do.

Going Further: Getting Competitive with Yourself

The first month of my Spending Fast was great. I had proven to myself that I did in fact have money to pay off my debt, and I was so happy that I'd set myself up to fix my mess of a financial situation. That first month, by spending money on Needs Only, I was amazed to discover that I had $505.58 left over to send to the first creditor on my Debt Hit List. Before the Spending Fast, I was bouncing checks, racking up overdraft fees, and ending the month without a cent to my name. Now, faced with this self-generated "windfall," I couldn't believe I'd spent the last nine years telling myself I had no money to pay off my debt. I'd been motivated by desperation and energized by the novelty of my experiment. I was transforming from mild-mannered government clerk by day to debt-paying-off badass kingpin by night. I didn't want to lose momentum, so I started to think about how I could keep moving forward. Was there a way to take the Spending Fast to another level to pay off even more debt? This is when I realized I was going to have a contest *with myself*.

Getting competitive with yourself means taking a look at how your actions and decisions have a direct impact on the amount you can pay to the top account on your Debt Hit List. It's about finding a way to beat your own personal best each month. A weightlifter has a max he or she has ever lifted; why not see how much money you can send to your bills? You've got to find your inner badass and be willing to go all in to beat your personal record.

I got creative with my thinking. I reanalyzed every part of my spending and non-spending. I started to think about how I could manage to get more income, so that my debt would shrink sooner. I began to really understand that my past attempts at paying off debt hadn't worked because the amount I was saving and then sending off to my creditors was so paltry. By eliminating money spent on Wants, I was able to pay off a huge amount of debt right away. It was quick and exciting, and I was anxious to see how far I could take it. The second month of the Spending Fast I almost doubled the first month's savings, paying off $934.95 in debt! I had set a new personal best, but I was determined to do even better. Yet another mission emerged: *How can I take this to the next level so I can pay off even more?*

I was constantly thinking about what purchases I could cut. I dug deeper and found little ways to save even more money. On the way to my job I would take the travel mug I had found in the Lost and Found box at work and stop by my gym to fill up on free coffee that was set out in the lobby (I admit that I even pocketed a few free tea bags on occasion). I realized the bits of lipstick I dug out of the bottom of the tube worked just as well as if I'd bought a fresh one. I even combined all the last slivers of soap into one Frankenstein-esque bar. It was still soap, and it worked just as well. Making a commitment to get competitive with yourself is a great way to reenergize your Spending Fast. Congratulate yourself for all the money you've sent off to your creditors, but take a few minutes to ask yourself the following questions:

What other expenses can I cut out of my life? Is everything on the Needs side still really a Need?

Now that I've seen how amazing I am at getting things cheaper, are there other items on my Needs list I can get for less?

Am I getting my money's worth out of all the stuff on my Needs list? For example, am I going to the gym enough to warrant that monthly fee? Can I try living without Internet access for three months? Or could I go without any processed food? What about becoming a freegan (someone who rejects consumerism by using discarded food and other goods)? Or renting out our entire house while living in an Airstream (or other less expensive alternative housing)? What else can I do without?

You may well be thinking, *I've already stopped buying everything I could think of when I made my Wants and Needs List. Seriously, you want me to do more?* I'm not saying you have to take extreme measures and get five roommates or start hitchhiking to work, but dig deeper than you have previously. This stage is all about ratcheting your efforts up to the next level so your debt removal gets a supercharge.

While I definitely think you should be proud of every bit of progress you make, I also encourage you to take it up a couple notches.

My husband and I had been doing well with our Spending Fast, and had been doing a good job of sticking to Needs-Only spending. One of the items we kept on the Needs side of our list were family outings. We felt we'd probably lose our minds if we couldn't do fun stuff with our two small children. We found lots of free activities, but decided that once a month we could do an all-day outing, which usually involved going into the city, doing an activity, and probably having brunch. While we saved lots of money limiting these kinds of activities to once a month, we realized we could do more.

Last week's activity was a great example. We had our two kids in the car and they were going stir crazy, so it was really tempting to pay a whopping $20 to park (it's not easy parking in New York City). We decided to be patient and drive around a little more, when a spot on the street opened up. We spent a total of $2 on parking. When it was time for brunch, and our kids were starving, we went into the first fun-looking restaurant that didn't have a line out to the sidewalk. We got a table, got menus, and realized it was a mistake to not look at the prices before sitting down. Kids' chicken fingers were $14. Seriously? We got up, went across the street to Chipotle, and ate for a fraction of the price. We probably saved nearly $100 by being more patient and making decisions that resulted in our spending a lot less. We're really excited to have even more money to put toward my student loan this month. This experience energized us to see what else we can do more cheaply and to try to beat our personal best each month.   —Taylor

(Semi- and Completely) Shameless Frugal Ways to Save Even More Money

Unplug your gadgets and small appliances to eliminate "vampire power." (Appliances draw energy just by being plugged in. You don't even have to actually be using them for them to cost you money.)

When it's time to replace lightbulbs, switch to compact fluorescents.

Go completely TV-free. Write, read, paint, or work instead.

Eat substantially less meat.

Turn down the heat and pile on the layers.

Use a clothesline, even inside, to dry clothing.

Wash and reuse plastic baggies.

Reuse your dental floss (with a good rinse it'll be good as new).

Cut open the toothpaste tube to get every last bit.

Ask your friends for their leftovers.

Sell the majority of your things and become a professional couch surfer (find out more on Couchsurfing.org).

It's gross to think about, but flush your toilet less often (that is, when you don't leave behind solids). Some drought-stricken regions already suggest this habit.

Don't be afraid to eat foods three to five days past their expiration date. (Use the information at StillTasty.com to find out if you should keep it or toss it.)

Rather than dump the assorted bits of food that don't get eaten by each family member into the trash, combine it all in a reusable container and eat it the next day.

Dumpster-dive at work. Pull discarded Starbucks coffee bags out of the trash. When you bring them into the store you can trade the bag for a free tall coffee.

When eating out, always take home your leftovers, no matter how small the portions.

Wear your clothing more often between washes.

Every once in a while, wear your dirty clothes right into the shower so they get a good rinse; squeeze the water out and hang them to dry. (Skip the jeans on this tip. Trying to wiggle out of drenched jeans isn't worth the headache.)

Take extremely fast showers and don't turn up the hot water.

Put buckets in your shower and use the extra water (called greywater) for other nondrinking purposes around the house.

Reuse the liner from cereal boxes as a waxed paper substitute.

Wash your clothes only in cold water.

Stuff more laundry into each load to cut down on the total number of loads. But avoid overloading the washing machine!

Use one-third of the recommended amount of shampoo, conditioner, toothpaste, dishwasher, and laundry detergent.

Wash your hair less often. Embrace the sexy/dirty look. (Hairdressers always say that's the best way to keep hair healthy anyway.)

Sell your car and don't look back.

Always ask for a lower price even if it's not a traditional negotiating situation.

Resist the urge to be blond if you're naturally brunette. A shade closer to your natural hair color requires less maintenance. Not having to cover up those roots as often can save you over $1,500 a year!

Take on a roommate (or two) to cut down on housing expenses.

Have college students who are learning a trade cut your hair, clean your teeth, or provide therapy sessions.

Resolve to never buy new.

Ask when the stuff in the lost and found box at your office, gym, or apartment building will get thrown out. See if there's anything you need from what has been unclaimed. Airports' unclaimed luggage auctions offer especially good finds.

If you are a woman, do not buy gender-specific items, such as shaving cream in a pink or purple container. Products marketed toward women can be marked up as much as 70 percent over equivalent items for men.

If you love pumpkin spice lattes or other flavored lattes, save 50 percent by getting a regular coffee with pumpkin or vanilla (or whatever flavor you like) syrup added.

Create a uniform for yourself. Add variety to it with accessories. Sell the rest of your clothes.

Unsubscribe to store e-mail lists or have the solicitations sent to your spam folder. Who needs the temptation?

You need to decide which methods of cutting back further are right for you. The most important thing is that you keep at it, and continue to evaluate every area of your spending. I did a few unconventional things during this stage, but I believe getting competitive with myself made a difference. Here are some examples of what I did during that time:

Switched to a smaller and cheaper locker at the gym. Savings: $4 per month

Found a cheaper face wash. Savings: $7 per month

Drank coffee away from home only when I found it for free. Savings: incalculable!

Swiped (and then returned) old magazines from the gym. Savings: approximately $3.50 per magazine

Made homemade notepads out of scrap paper. Savings: $3 each

Ate exclusively out of my canned soup collection. Savings: $3 each

I want you to look at every expense with a skeptical eye and with the assumption that you've been overpaying. I'll be the first to admit that these are small amounts of money in some cases. Just trust me when I tell you that cumulative efforts ultimately make a big difference. Getting competitive with yourself and making sacrifices presents yet another challenge in this getting-out-of-debt business, but keep in mind that the more you save, the faster you'll get there. Get creative and stay focused on the final goal.

$ Let's Do This!

- ❑ Make decisions about how you want to spend your new newfound free time.
- ❑ Don't be afraid to tell people you're on a Spending Fast and the reason you're doing it.
- ❑ Use the Spending Fast as your "bad guy"/scapegoat/excuse to get yourself out of spendy activities.
- ❑ Compete with yourself to beat your own personal savings record.
- ❑ Reanalyze your Wants and Needs List. Are there any Needs you can do without?

CHAPTER 9

Generating Additional Income: Finding New Gigs

At this stage in the Spending Fast I was really pleased with my progress. I'd paid off more debt than I had expected, I was making permanent and positive changes, and I was getting really excited about cutting out even more expenses. But I wasn't just thinking about what else I could cut out. I was opening up time—by not stressing about paying bills and not running around to stores charging up bags' worth of stuff. I had time to home in on my skills, talents, and interests—and I started to think about what else I could do to generate more income. I was determined to bring more money into my life and get out of debt even faster.

Show Me the Money: Additional Income Streams

I was well on my way to permanently crushing my autopilot spending habits, so adding more income was going to make me unstoppable in my mission to get out of debt. Initially, I thought this sounded impossible, because I was already working forty hours a week. Ultimately it came down to getting creative about incorporating an additional income stream into my life. I knew the ideal scenario would be generating income in a way that would fit into my existing schedule without much effort. In the spirit of the Spending Fast, I focused on the fact that I was *capable,* and that *any-*

thing was possible if I decided it was. I didn't need someone to offer me a position or validate that I was capable. I was going to have confidence in my abilities, and know others would follow suit.

My two main criteria for adding an income stream into my life were *time* and *opportunity*. I didn't want to be overwhelmed by another responsibility. I wanted it to feel like I was adding an opportunity to my life, not creating a chore. I wanted to utilize my skills to do something I enjoyed during my free time and get paid for it too.

Time

Whatever I landed on needed to fit into my life without much effort. I wasn't interested in working 24/7, getting no sleep, or being super stressed out. Free time had opened up so much once I stopped spending money on superfluous stuff: I was no longer passing time shopping online, browsing every chance I got, or packing up returns. The amount of time I wasted with my spending was shocking to me. You, too, may be using way more time than you realize bringing those items you don't need into your life.

I started to think about uncommitted chunks of time I had in my schedule. I was working from 8 to 5, Monday through Friday, but I had an unusually long lunch break. It was 1.5 hours, and it was just waiting to get maximized!

Before the Spending Fast, I would go to yoga after work, and I did random stuff on weekends: shopping, hanging out with friends, spending time with Aaron, partying, and so on. After carefully examining my schedule for pockets of time, I saw that I had time open in the evenings, and I could definitely fit something in on weekends if I wanted to. I also knew it would be easy to utilize my lunch break more effectively. I realized that for me, getting a regularly scheduled part-time job wouldn't have been the best fit. I needed to make more money during the free time I had here and there. Plus, I didn't feel I needed to earn thousands of dollars on the side for whatever I did for it to be worth it. I love mottoes, so for this stage of the Spending Fast my motto became "Any money is good money, even if it isn't much money." This line of thinking made me believe that generating more income was possible—I didn't feel defeated by the time restraints of my full-time job.

Opportunity

I wanted to make use of the particular set of skills I have—I'm crafty and I'm a photographer. While these are skills, I also *enjoy* taking pictures and creating things. It was important to me that I utilize these strengths when creating an opportunity to bring in more money. I asked myself a few questions that helped me think about what I could actually do. What was I good at? Photography and crafting. What did I like to do? Photography, crafts, baking, exercising, shopping (obviously), and zoning out looking at Pinterest. How did I like to help people? By documenting their lives, giving them something tangible to look back on. What did I enjoy doing before I had to make a living? When I was younger I loved taking pictures (again with the pictures), playing sports, going to camp, canoeing, making crafts (yes, seeing a theme here), making home movies, running through the sewer (don't ask), riding my bike on a dirt path through the woods, and eating Swiss Cake Rolls.

Love of Crafts and Photography = More Money

While I initially wasn't sure *exactly* what I should do to earn extra income, it quickly became clear that crafting and photography were viable options. What could I make that people would want? How could I use my photography talent? Even though I went to photography school, I wasn't using photography as a way to make money, and as much as I wished eating Swiss Cake Rolls while browsing the Internet was a valid way to earn money, it was not. I started to brainstorm about how I could turn crafting and photography into income streams. After some serious thinking, I opened a virtual shop called Anna Made It. The name was intentionally vague, so I could sell whatever I wanted without being confined to specific goods. Over the entire time I sold my creations on Etsy (2010–2013), I managed to make—wait for it—$4,260.37. Everything was made completely in my spare time, and in addition to my regular full-time day job.

I was enjoying what I was doing. Some of the things I made were baby onesies with phrases on them like BABY GOT BACK, HALF PIRANHA/HALF ANGEL, 9 MONTHS AGO I HAD A TAIL, SHORT STACK, and even RAISED BY SQUIRRELS. I don't know what that last one meant, but it was just strange enough to get people's attention, and it sold. I also designed and made shipping labels, calendars, and stickers.

Opening and operating an online shop and sticking to the Spending Fast took some planning. I had to run the shop in a way that involved no overhead. Other than the listing fee of twenty cents, I didn't shell out any money to get started. I made the decision early to sell things that didn't require me to buy materials in advance, and I bought supplies only when orders came in. I generated all the onesie ideas in Photoshop, so buyers could see what they would look like without my having to make samples—which would have required buying materials to make. An advantage to working this way was that I could basically make up a new design and toss it on the site, and if it didn't sell it didn't cost me. I was only out the twenty-cent listing fee and the time I spent working on the design. I gave my onesies a price I considered really expensive at the time—$15—considering that they cost me about $3 to make. (Now that I have a baby of my own, I know that's actually pretty reasonable for kids' clothes.) I remember thinking, *What the hell are people doing spending this kind of money on a onesie?!* Then I remembered, *Oh yeah, that used to be me.*

I knew I wasn't fully tapping into my skills as a photographer, so I started to think about how I could make money with my talent. Years earlier, I'd shot weddings by myself, using real film. I developed every roll and contact sheet by hand and made all the prints myself. I usually shot at least fifteen rolls per wedding. At the time, I didn't have a car, so I was using public transportation and renting cars for the mountain-venue weddings. While a heavy workload and stressful situations don't scare me off easily, this routine burned me out quickly. I went on an approximately five-year hiatus from weddings.

When I was thinking about how to increase my income, Aaron suggested we try shooting weddings together. I was reluctant at first, since I had only my previous arduous wedding experiences as a reference point, but the Spending Fast made me look at things with an open mind. It was clear right away that shooting digital and having access to a car (Aaron's) was going to make wedding photography much easier and far more enjoyable. We started telling everyone we knew about our wedding photography business. It started slowly, but it grew by word of mouth and we got busier. We used money we made from booking weddings to grow the business and slowly buy newer and better equipment. Even though I was on the Spending

Fast, I naturally wanted to go big and get everything right away. (The photography business expenses were not considered my personal expenses, and its finances were completely separate from my own.) Aaron was the voice of reason, as usual. Eventually we were able to take a nice percentage from each portrait session and wedding to supplement our day-job incomes. Eight months in, we booked a wedding on Martha's Vineyard. I remember how ironic it felt to be in the middle of all that luxury when I was living a bare-bones existence back home. I'm grateful to have found success with wedding photography, and this is yet another example of how the Spending Fast brought more good things into my life. Eventually I even figured out how to apply for a public art commission, which I ended up getting.

While I won't pretend it was easy figuring out how to translate skills into money, I know I wouldn't have pushed myself to try if I hadn't been seeking ways to earn more. I was comfortable with my job at the courthouse. The judge I worked for was kind. I was also making a steady income, and I had good benefits. Prior to the Spending Fast, there had been no reason to seriously consider ever leaving my position. While working in a courtroom wasn't my dream job by any means, it *did* have its interesting moments, such as hearing heartbreaking and eye-opening victim impact statements at sentencings, and there was also that time when a shackled inmate barreled through a third-floor glass window in an attempt to escape his incarceration. It was a while before I tackled my biggest hurdle, but eventually my commitment to the Spending Fast and my determination to live an autonomous life brought me to where I am today. I left my courthouse job and now have a flexible schedule while making money doing what I *love* doing: photography. It's only because I made the changes necessary to become debt-free that today I'm able to have the choices I do.

Turning Passions into Moneymakers

I am grateful that it wasn't too big of a challenge to discover what I liked to do—and to transition those passions into moneymaking gigs. I want to be clear that it's okay if you don't figure out immediately what will work for you. It's important that you take the time to cook up some thoughts. Screw being humble—be honest; what are you really good at? Ask your friends and family to name your special talents. Ask on Facebook. It's not uncommon for other people to have extra insight about what we're good at that we can't see. Lots of times I'll be able to see ways a person could make money because I can see the person's own skills and talents in a way he or she can't. Sometimes you're just too close to see things clearly.

It's entirely possible that the perfect side job has been right under your nose all along, but you just might not have been able to see it. Answer the following questions to the best of your ability, coming up with at least three answers for the first four questions. Go for it, don't be shy or worry about being humble. You're not going to figure out what you're good at unless you're willing to put yourself out there and be honest about what you're awesome at.

Ask yourself:

> What am I good at? What do I do well and what special skills do I have?
> What are my best characteristics and traits?
> What are my favorite things to do?
> How do I spend my time when I'm away from my regular job?
> What do I like to do?
> Do I have any skills that aren't being fully utilized?
> Could any of my skills be useful to others?
> What did I like to do when I was a kid?
> What have I thought about doing to make extra money but haven't pursued yet?
> My dream job would be_____.
> What's my current work schedule?

Next, ask important people in your life what you're good at and note common themes.

The answers to these questions will give you insights into different areas that you can consider exploring to make extra money. For example, let's say you answered that you're precise, organized, and creative, and some of your best qualities are that you're responsible, detail-oriented, and outgoing. And wow, it turns out you like to make illustrations and greeting cards. You could provide a seasonal gift-wrapping service featuring hand-crafted cards and "artisan" wrapping paper. Cha-ching.

Maybe you're strong, patient, and nurturing—and outdoorsy, compassionate and understanding. You love playing with your dog and your friends' dogs, and hanging out at the dog park. *You are all about dogs.* Hello, dog-walking service.

Keep reminding yourself: A*ny money is good money.* If you're creating an opportunity for yourself that's not going to cause major stress, *any money* that you bring in will help you get rid of the debt faster. Don't disregard a moneymaking opportunity just because it isn't going to immediately bring in thousands of dollars.

Blogging for Cold Hard Cash

While I certainly don't think a blog is the answer for everyone, it's definitely a viable option for some. I'm often asked how to make money from blogging, and I'm happy to share a few things about what I've learned. Let's come up with an awesome fictional person who, for the purposes of this exercise, just so happens to have a lot in common with my husband, Aaron (who is also awesome). Let's walk through what this person said on the Turning Passions into Money questionnaire. I really want you to see that no matter how random your passions, skills, and qualities may appear to be, there's a way to create a moneymaking operation based on what you're good at.

Fictional Potential Blogger Said

He's good at: bowling, reading maps, and remembering movie facts.

The best things about him are: he's funny, he's always on time, and he can travel anywhere without getting lost.

His favorite things to do are: hang out with adorable son, sleep, go to the movies, run, travel, get tattoos, read, and eat ice cream.

How he spends his time when not at his regular job: see previous answers, plus cleaning, grocery shopping, working out, hanging out with friends, Face-Timing with out-of-state family, doing photography jobs (weddings, families, babies, anything).

What he's thought about doing to make money but hasn't pursued: graphic design (would love to take a class), website coding.

His dream job: movie reviewer.

His current work schedule: Monday through Friday, 8:30 a.m. to 5:00 p.m., with photography gigs on the weekends and photography business meetings with clients in the evenings.

What This Fictional Potential Blogger Could Do

This person can handle a lot—he's working full-time, exercising, managing free-lance jobs on weekends, and raising a child. Blogs require more time than you would think. This person is also "funny," "reads," and "likes to see movies." He's interested in graphic design and coding, major bonus skills if you want to start a blog. And his dream job is to be a movie reviewer? I could see a movie review blog or website in this awesome fictional person's future. How would that work?

The Setup

A movie review blog could focus on movies that are available on Netflix or from Redbox, so people don't have to spend extra money on movie tickets. The site could be set up relatively inexpensively, and there's pretty much no overhead. Having coding skills will prevent him from having to hire outside help to get the site started. Until our blogger develops his own graphic design skills, he can utilize one of the many free, beautiful premade website templates available online. Later on, the graphic design skills he's honed will come in handy when he updates the blog's design. This person is funny and has a great memory for movie details, and that's going to make this an enjoyable venture.

Blogs Are Flexible

A blog can be worked on early in the morning before work, in the evenings, and on weekends. The great thing about a blog is that you can work around your own schedule. Our blogger can do one of his favorite activities—watching movies—to develop the content for the blog. Another way blogs are flexible is that you can post whenever you want (although you gotta be consistent if you want people to read it), and you can even write pieces in advance and post later depending on your other responsibilities. And of course you can work on your blog anywhere that you can bring a tablet or laptop—or even borrow someone else's computer if needed.

Where the Money Comes From

Blogs and websites make money in many different ways. For the purposes of this example, I'm going to focus on two income streams: advertising and affiliate marketing. With advertising, bloggers can place a traditional ad anywhere on their site. Or the advertiser can pay a set amount for a post about their brand, company, or product. Sometimes advertisers will pay to have the blogger simply wear the item or mention it and link it to the advertiser. With affiliate marketing, a link is placed on the blog within a word or phrase. The affiliate link is associated with the blog. If a reader of the blog clicks on that link, then the advertiser pays the blogger a fee. Sometimes bloggers make a percentage based on each sale and sometimes it's a set amount. Google Adsense and Amazon Associates are some of the easiest affiliate programs to set up and use.

Once the site has picked up steam, it would even be possible to use reviews written for the blog as writing samples to submit to writing jobs at different papers and magazines, and maybe bigger movie review sites and blogs.

There Are Lots of Options

I'm sure some of you are thinking, *Um, yeah. Who doesn't want to be a movie reviewer?!* Now, don't be a buzzkill and start shooting down ideas before you even get going.

The point of this exercise is to get you thinking about ideas. Make a list of all the options that come to mind. At this point, don't think about being practical, or get yourself weighed down by logistics when you're in this considering-all-possibilities stage. Even if you find yourself thinking about something seemingly random or unrelated to any of your skills, include it. Write it down. You never know, you could find yourself earning extra cash by selling sweet frozen goodies out of one of those little carts, walking around the neighborhood dinging your heart away with that bell. Crazier things have happened. Also—and keep this in mind—with anything you're considering doing, you don't have to be an expert to get started. If you're good at what you do and you have confidence in your skills, others will too.

Everything Doesn't Have to Be the Best-Case Scenario, Though

While we're on the topic of selling frozen treats, I'll admit it would definitely be the best-case scenario to find a side gig that utilizes your talents and honors your passions. However, don't eliminate moneymaking options because they don't seem to fit in with your skills or long-term goals. Sometimes you just gotta make a buck the way you gotta make a buck. While I truly believe anyone can eventually find a way to use individual talents to make money, I don't want to lose sight of the biggest goal: getting out of debt as fast as possible. Should you decide that it's not the right time for you to figure out your dream side gig, that's *fine*. If you find yourself taking a decidedly unglamorous job to earn extra cash, just remember that it's temporary.

The Part-Time Job

An official part-time job is an option too. If you're still sorting out what you're good at and want to do as your extra gig, or feeling uninspired, a more traditional part-time position may be the good route to take. While coming up with random freelance gigs worked for me, this solution is not necessarily for everyone. If you can be available for consistent slots of time, working for someone else might be a great solution. Just think carefully about what the job entails to make sure it will support your commitment to the Spending Fast. Before my Fast I tried to get a part-time seasonal job at the Gap to pay down my debt. I was planning to work there after finishing my day job, and would have worked from five-thirty to close. But during the interview, I kept thinking about all the cute stuff I would probably, most definitely need to buy. It was a blessing in disguise that I didn't get that position, because chances are I would have been spending my valuable time digging myself deeper into debt.

While a part-time job may be great for you, think twice if it's the kind of job that's going to rekindle your autopilot spending habits. There are lots of part-time jobs that won't put you in a position to be tempted to spend. Some of the side jobs that fall into the part-time, freelance, safe-from-spending variety are:

Cleaning houses

Babysitting/being a nanny (pitching yourself to overworked parents for overnight or evening shifts can turn into a big moneymaker)

Housesitting/caretaking

Renting out your home or a room in your residence (read more online at Airbnb.com or HomeAway.com)

Driving for Uber or Lyft

Temping

Working as a waiter for a caterer

Dog walking

Event planning (again, target exhausted parents—plan kids' parties with cool themes, specially designed invitations, creative decorations, fun games, and snacks and cakes)

Gardening and yard work

Helping people pack, move, and unpack

Painting home interiors

Working as a personal assistant/errand runner

Working as a shot girl/bartender

Tutoring

Working as a virtual assistant (someone who is usually self-employed who
provides professional, administrative, technical, or creative/social
assistance to clients remotely from a home office)
Writing and editing résumés

DO OTHERS WANT TO KNOW WHAT YOU KNOW?

Many communities offer continuing education classes for adults at colleges, universities, and recreation centers. Do you have a skill that you can teach to others? Do you speak a foreign language fluently? Are you a natural at public speaking? Do you know how to reupholster furniture, or are you a natural at improvisation? Check out the offerings in your community, or pitch the idea of a class to a store or other establishment. Maybe there's a nearby knitting store that needs an instructor. Or maybe you could start an improv class at a neighborhood bar. Tutoring is an option too. If you're great at calculus or are a skilled writer, market yourself as a tutor to high school or college students.

SUBJECT: Should I spend money to make money?

Hey Anna,

I'm trying to get a job as a display coordinator at Anthropologie. I'm praying they like my portfolio. I interviewed for a sales position as a way into the company. With a sales job comes . . . discounts. While that's great, I am over $20,000 in debt (and I share a loan with my mom that is more than twice that). How can I look like I belong at Anthropologie when I can't afford to work there? I get that they are selling a lifestyle, but even the clothes that are on sale are out of my budget. What should I do?

As you may guess from reading this book thus far, I am not a fan of spending money to make money. This practice has the potential to throw you right back into the autopilot spending that got you into debt in the first place. If a job needs an investment from you to get you going, think about how you can avoid the costs. I'm all for faking the look so that you can take the job, as long as you think you can avoid temptation to spend your paycheck on clothes from the store. Dissect the outfits and figure out what it is that gives them that certain look. Anthropologie does a lot of layering, muted colors, and mixing and matching of fabrics and textures. Figure out what less expensive pieces (or better yet, ones you already own) you can find at the thrift store or borrow from friends to create a similar look. While the sales rack items may still be too pricey, check out on-sale accessories. You might be able to nab a few of those to make your outfits pass the test.

Finding the Gigs

To find the customers for your side job, just start putting the word out. Tell your friends and family you're looking to do odd jobs or whatever it is you have come up with. You never know when someone is going to need a professional house sitter, or need to have a few rooms painted. Get the word out to a group of people that you're available to clean out garages and organize offices. Before you know it, you'll be earning the extra cash that puts you closer to paying off your debts.

Let's Do This!

- ❏ Figure out when you have blocks of uncommitted time.
- ❏ Make a list of any moneymaking possibilities, both glamorous and unglamorous.
- ❏ Narrow down your list to the jobs you would enjoy doing and could realistically make happen within the time you have available.
- ❏ Network with absolutely everyone you know until you snag a lead.

FiLL YouR LiFE WiTH ONLY tHE itEMS, PEOPLE, tAsKS, & tEcHNoLoGiES tHAt PosiTiVELY AFFECT YOU. EVERythiNG ELSE MUST GO.

CHAPTER 10

Turning Stuff You Don't Want into Cash

Side gigs and freelance work are a great way to earn more money to put toward your debt. I was really focused on getting through my Debt Hit List as soon as possible, so I got to thinking that the pile of crap that got me into debt in the first place could be part of my ticket out. While getting rid of things was another way to have more income flowing into my account, there were other benefits to selling my stuff. Cutting down on the excess supports your newfound commitment to a debt-free life in a few ways. First, you can get money for things that are no longer of use to you. Second, it can be nice having less clutter laying around—spaces feel lighter. And last, you're going to see how having too much stuff complicates life. Accumulating belongings costs you not only money but also energy and time.

When you start questioning the purpose (Does this item still meet my needs?) or necessity of everything you've chosen to bring into your life, buying for the sake of buying becomes way less appealing. When you're aware of what's driving your decision making, you'll buy only items that enhance and support your life. And, of course, the less you seek to accumulate, the less you'll spend. The unspent money can be used in a more purposeful and conscious way: to pay off debt, start a savings account, build a down payment toward a home, further your education, or help a charity or good cause you're passionate about, or maybe you'll use it to travel more, as you always wished you could.

Start Easy

Sometimes, figuring out what to get rid of and sell is tough. What if you get rid of something you'll need later? What if you regret throwing something out? Having a sentimental attachment to items is common. Objects can hold emotions. How could you toss the shirt you wore when you met your soul mate? But what if you tell yourself that everything you own is an *essential* item? It's not as if the bent butter knife that's just sitting in a drawer is somehow a key component to your kitchen's overall efficiency.

To overcome your emotional attachment to belongings, start by getting rid of items that you obviously no longer need or want: that bag of feathers you bought for craft projects but haven't touched in years, that shirt you know you could look great in (but don't), and that old laptop you're sure could still be useful to someone (but not you). I could go on. The point is, some things will be easier to part with than others. Make it easy for yourself by starting with items you're less attached to, and work up to the tougher decisions.

Cabinets, Crannies, Nooks, and Other Forgotten Places

Go to the places in your home where all the unused things tend to gravitate. You know where I mean: the back of the closets, the shelves in the garage, the storage containers in the basement, under the bed, or in the lower furniture drawers. Here you're most likely to find a gathering of things that are no longer serving you. Maybe you stashed stuff away because you had planned on dealing with it later, or you're sick of looking at it for the time being. Maybe you thought a particular item would come in handy someday, or you're saving it for someone who can get some use out of it. The back of my closet is apparently where I shoved all the stuff I didn't want to deal with. I found a lot of things to get rid of. One might say I liked the *idea* of these things more than the *reality* of them. Here's are some of the things I sold, gave away, donated, recycled, or tossed:

An old laptop
Two rugs
Three boxes of tea (I'm an aspirational tea drinker.)

A large bag of miniature soaps, shampoos, and conditioners (gathered from loved ones who wanted to help me save money). My inner cheapskate wanted to keep them, but I knew that I could donate them to a place that needed them more than I did.

Many clothes (I gave myself permission to let go of the clothes that I was hoarding year after year with the hope that someday I would wear them again but never did.)

Digging Deeper

After you've done a clean sweep of the unused things you've been hanging on to, check out what else you have on hand that you don't love, use, need, or want. This stuff may be sitting in plain sight, or you might have to whittle down collections that are getting out of control. For me, digging deeper meant going through my closet (not the back, but the everyday clothes hanging in front of my face) and our craft room/office/catch-all room again, and doing a visual sweep of the things that were out and about in our living spaces while asking myself at each item I came across, *But do I love it?* This is in the same vein as Marie Kondo's question, "Does this item spark joy?" In the process of digging deeper, I revealed that I had a busted humidifier and a bag of Epsom salts tucked under the kitchen sink, more than my fair share of crafting supplies, stacks of old magazines I was intending to reference for something someday, and too many pairs of sunglasses that made me look like the rapper I wasn't. While this process is about finally deciding to rid yourself of the hodgepodge of coffee mugs you inherited from your college roommate, it's also about making tougher choices.

For example, I have a friend who's an academic and naturally he reads a lot. Over time he's managed to amass a pretty extensive book collection, but frankly it was getting out of control. He had so many books that they were piling up everywhere, and they were beginning to take over the living room. When he wanted to access a particular one, it was nearly impossible to find. He knew that if his collection kept growing at this rate, he was going to have to start charging it rent. He went through his books carefully one by one, deciding which ones he really wanted to keep. At the end, he was left with a meticulously curated collection of the books that were the most useful to him.

This stage was harder for me. I actually had trouble getting rid of a bag of over a hundred clothespins that I *knew* I would need someday. Plus, it just felt wasteful to get rid of something that worked perfectly fine, only to open up the possibility of having to purchase a replacement later.

Eventually, not a single corner of my home was untouched. I went through everything, cleaning and organizing as I went. The wildest part, though, is that I don't miss any of it. Even better, I was able to turn those items into cash by selling them, which I'll discuss in more detail in the next section.

How to Prepare Your Junk—and Yourself—for Selling

As I went through my living space and found items I didn't want to keep, I divided them into five categories: Sell, Trash, Donate, Recycle, and Give Away. Here's a sampling of stuff I put on my Sell list.

Mop head
Humidifier
Books
Gel eye mask
Sunglasses
Package of chai tea
Baby headband
Half-full canister of powdered hot chocolate mix
Accordion fan
Kiddie stickers
Almost full bag of Epsom salts
Large bag of clothespins
Clothes
Sneakers
Tin box

When it comes to selling the stuff you don't want, there are a few ways to do it. If you have the time to devote to trying to get as much money as possible for your stuff, great, go for it. List every item on Craigslist or eBay, field every inquiry, and wait until you find a buyer willing to pay your highest price. Hold out for the most money you can get.

If you value your time more than the dollars you could be making, you might want to consider the approach I took. I wasn't picky about how I was going to get rid of the stuff; I wanted it out of my life no matter what. Making the most money off my junk while being efficient with my time was what I was after. This method definitely isn't about hauling in the maximum amount of money, but I also didn't want to spend any more time dealing with my junk. I had spent enough time going through it all already and I was ready to move on. Here are the guidelines I followed:

Touch items only once. When you make the decision to get rid of something, stick it in a box or bag and leave it there. Don't use up time and energy moving things from spot to spot.

Consolidate your efforts. Avoid time-wasters like listing *one* thing on Craigslist at a time. List your red retro stapler and Western-style belt buckle consecutively. Take your photos and make your listings all at once. Think assembly line.

Distinguish between high and low value. Generally speaking, electronics, furniture, photographic equipment, and vintage or designer items have the most value in the resale world. Things that have less value: clothes, knickknacks, and everyday items such as utensils, plates, organizational bins, and common home goods. Devote more time and attention to the items with the higher earning potential, and less to the others.

Detach. People don't pay extra because an item is meaningful to you or because it was given to you with love. If you're ready to part with things, separate the meaning and memories from them. That said, I'm not telling you to dig out your mom's wedding dress because it might bring in some cash. If you don't particularly care for something but you're keeping it because you'd feel guilty getting rid of it right then, hold off and revisit the idea of letting it go in a few months.

Where to Sell: Yard Sales, Listservs, and More

Now that you've done the hard work of clearing out the stuff you don't want, you've got to decide on your venue for getting rid of it. There are several good options; decide which one works best for you.

The Classic Yard Sale

I felt my best chances of making the most money in the least amount of time and effort was to hold a good ol' yard sale. I liked that I could try to sell my stuff all at once, rather than bothering to list items individually online or take them to consignment shops. I happen to think it doesn't hurt to try to sell absolutely everything. On a whim I put out used makeup, thinking that doing so was kind of gross and possibly, most definitely unhygienic, but figured, *What the hell. I'll just set it out and see what happens.* Hours later, I was shocked to have someone handing me money for my old, albeit practically untouched lipstick. Even if I did make only a quarter off it, that's more than I had before the sale, so it was fine with me. Be bold and put everything out—you just don't know who might walk by and think, *Hey, it's my lucky day. I have fifty cents I've been looking to spend and this half-used packet of chai tea is just the thing for me.* (This actually happened.) Try to sell as much as you possibly can. As I mentioned earlier, one of my rules was: *Once it leaves the house, it isn't coming back in.* This meant I really wanted to make sure as much stuff moved as possible. There are some techniques you can follow to get the most out of your yard sale. Most of them boil down to using attractive displays to suck customers in and setting good prices to get them to part with their money.

Your Inner Stylist

Now let's be real: I'm not talking about taking weeks to plan the layout and placement of each random coffee cup and tattered paperback. But it's a good idea to display things in a manner that's eye-catching and makes it easy for the customer to see your goods. If you pile everything up on a table, it looks like a big heap of junk (okay, it might actually *be* a pile of junk, but for the sake of the yard sale, let's try to elevate the junk at least to the level of *respectable* junk). I hung the clothes for sale on a clothesline, where they looked cute and were easy for people passing by to see. One of the girls who stopped by actually said, "I don't know if it's because of how they're displayed or what, but I want to buy them all." I definitely sold more clothes than I would have if they'd been in a giant mound that people had to wade through. Because the clothes were selling quickly, I was sure to constantly restock the line, tidying up when things were starting to look too sloppy. Conveniently, I was also selling several mirrors that were left over from a clothing swap I had. Having the mirrors on display near the clothesline made it easy for people to see how a particular piece of clothing would look on them, which led to more sales.

It was important that I took the time to really visualize what I wanted my yard sale to look like. I held the sale on a grassy area between hundred-year-old trees in front of our condo. It helped that it was also a perfect day—sunny, with just the right about of breeze. My husband helped me lug everything down two flights of stairs, and our son, Henry, even did his part by looking super-cute in his playpen. He attracted quite a few customers.

The takeaway here is that it's a good idea to create a welcoming layout at your yard sale. For example, if you have lots of jewelry to sell, pay attention to how you show it. Someone will be much more likely to buy a chunky necklace that they can get a good look at than one that's tangled up with a bracelet and an old phone charger. You don't have to make your display an elaborate, time-consuming ordeal—just make sure everything is as visible and as uncluttered-looking as possible.

Flip on the Sales Pitch

Obviously, the more stuff you get rid of, the more money you'll make—even if you don't get as much as you hoped for on every single item. When people were browsing at my yard sale I always walked up to them and flashed them my friendliest smile. I let them know that we were trying to get rid of absolutely everything, so we were offering great prices. This news got people's attention, and they seemed to look at things a little more closely once they knew they could get them for cheap. I was dishing out compliments left and right, even telling people what shirts would look good on them. When people left empty-handed I'd tell them, "Come by later on! We'll be out till five. Weather permitting, of course!" Insert a wink, chuckle, and pantomimed elbow jab. Used-car saleslady Anna was in full effect, laying it on thick: "We're liquidating! *Everything* must go!"

Don't Turn Down a Sale

Remember: Any money is good money. If someone offers you a dollar for a battered copy of *The Joy of Cooking* from 1986 that you think is worth two (because it is vintage), just take it. It's better to have a dollar than a book you haven't used since you wanted to make potato pancakes back in 2001.

Don't Put Prices on Everything

I didn't take the time to label anything with prices at my last yard sale. I figured in an effort to conserve time I'd just wing it, and I was nervous about how that'd go. You see, I grew up with a mom who really had her yard sale skills on point. I'm talking pro status. Days before her sale she'd dutifully get her permit, list the yard sale in the newspaper, and label each item with a price (in her delicate, perfect handwriting). She'd have plenty of change on hand—it is a cash business, after all. She'd set everything on the tables in the garage the night before and would start the sale promptly at the crack of dawn. I had big shoes to fill.

Needless to say, it felt slightly sacrilegious to not price things. When people asked me how much something was, I made up an amount and quickly spouted it out. For years, I had overthought the price tags. Not labeling gave me an opening to really go in for the kill when people were looking at certain things: "Isn't that shirt so cute!? Just $3!" Or: "I loved that book! For you? $1.50."

Details, Details

Speaking of permits, make sure you follow your town's rules for yard sales. If possible, hold your sale on a day where people are going to be out and about (weekends are obviously better). Don't stretch your sale out over multiple days. Devote one day to selling your stuff and then get back to your life.

Leftovers: Plan B

Right after the yard sale we divided the leftover stuff into a few categories: clothing/shoes/accessories, thrift store, bookstore, and donations. We decided we'd try to sell the wearables another way, so we brought those to a Buy-Sell-Trade store. The items the store didn't take we donated to the thrift store along with the unsold household and miscellaneous items. We tried to sell the books to the used book store, and the rest were given away as donations. Since I had worked so hard on purging, I was determined to not be left with boxes of things we just didn't need. In the end, here's how we made out:

> We earned $16.95 from the Buy-Sell-Trade store.
> The bookstore gave us a gift certificate for $19.25.
> Anything remaining was taken to a thrift store, and we got a donation receipt that will help out during tax time.

Overall we made $189.00 from the actual yard sale, which increased to $225.20 after we included the money we made from the Buy-Trade-Sell store and the bookstore credit. It wasn't the most profitable yard sale ever, but given that I made over $200 on stuff I would've gotten rid of anyway, and the whole process didn't take up too much of my time, I considered it a success. In addition to the extra income, it was also great to have less clutter in my home, and to be surrounded only by things I truly loved.

The Virtual Yard Sale

It's not possible for everyone to hold a yard sale. Things can get problematic if you live in an apartment with no yard and limited space, and if you do a big cleanout during the cold months you may not want to wait until spring to get your hands on that extra cash—or be stuck with stuff you already decided to purge. There are many different places to sell your things online. Here's a sampling:

Clothing: Poshmark.com, Threadflip.com, and Vinted.com

Jewelry: Exboyfriendjewelry.com

DVDs, CDs, and games: Decluttr.com

Kids' clothing, cloth diapers, craft supplies: VarageSale.com

Crafts, art, and sculpture: ArtPal.com and Etsy.com

Furniture, designer clothing, major electronics, appliances: eBay.com, Craigslist.org, and Backpage.com

Books: Cash4books.net

Wedding dresses: StillWhite.com

Smartphones, tablets, laptops, and computers: Gazelle.com

Tools, musical instruments, sporting goods: Amazon.com

Random items: Listia.com

Using Social Media to List Items

You can use Instagram (or any social media site for that matter) to hold a virtual garage sale. Keep in mind that with most online sales you'll need to have a PayPal account since it's one of the most popular and well-known ways to exchange money.

Also, on Instagram the majority of what I've seen for sale have been easily shippable items. For larger items such as motorcycles, people will specify "local pickup only."

If you're going to sell a lot of items and often, you'll want to set up a separate account to use specifically for selling, so you avoid spamming your regular followers with updates on your items for sale. (If you're selling an item only every once in a while, there's no need for a different account.) Take a quick (but well-lit) cell phone picture of each item for sale. Under each image, in the place for the caption, write something enticing about the item. A detailed description is great—stories are even better. For example: "Previous tour outfits, dresses, shoes, and jackets. These have been all over the world." What you write doesn't really matter, as long as it makes the item stand out. Naturally, you also need to list the terms of the sale, including information such as "1st person to leave PayPal e-mail address gets item. US only. Shipping included." The price should be listed under the picture of each item. It's also a good idea to include a hashtag so buyers can find your item even if they don't follow you. If you're selling clothes, be sure to include the hashtag #shopmycloset, so that people you don't know can find your auction. Right now there are over 1.5 million #shopmycloset hashtags on Instagram.

The "Auction" Technique

I've also seen some very popular bloggers, Instagrammers, and YouTubers hold auctions to sell their used things on Instagram. Creating a competitive environment sets up an opportunity for the seller to make even more money. To hold an online auction, decide on a time frame for the length of your sale—twenty-four to forty-eight hours works well. In the section on Instagram where you would typically write a witty blurb about yourself, explain the details of your auction instead, such as:

> *24-hour closet auction! Please leave your PayPal e-mail address in the comments. Shipping included in final bid. US only. Sorry, no returns.*

Take photographs of all your sale items and post them. Under each photo, write a description of the item: "Halter dress for sale. Size small, elastic in the back. Bidding starts at $23. Price includes shipping. US only. Leave a comment with your bid and PayPal e-mail address. Sale ends 2/19, 9:00 p.m. MST."

Promote Your Sale

Promote your Instagram sale on your personal Instagram feed, Facebook, Pinterest boards, and anywhere else you can think of. While there are lots of people shopping online, it's a good idea to make it as easy as possible for them to find your sale by announcing it everywhere you can.

Craigslist, Community E-mail Lists, and Local Facebook Groups

Craigslist is a great place to sell stuff you no longer want. First, it's got a huge user base and it's well known. People know that they can find just about anything on Craigslist, from a bicycle to an aquarium, so it's kind of a go-to place for people who like bargains. Craigslist charges no fees at all, so that's a huge plus. Listservs on community websites and Facebook groups are also becoming an increasingly accepted way to buy and sell. Check out the town or neighborhood where you live—it's entirely possible there's a whole website or Facebook group devoted to selling and buying stuff. A friend of mine who lives in the New York City area has practically furnished her entire house buying from her community e-mail list. Such places may be another great option for you to offload anything left over from a yard sale or midwinter purge.

Pawnshops

Pawnshops have been portrayed in a pretty shady light in movies and popular culture. They bring to mind some lonely, desperate person prying off her gold wedding band in the hope of pawning it for enough money to make her rent. But these shops are a solid option for getting rid of some items you know you don't want to keep. In a typical pawnshop deal, the shop gives out a loan (the interest rates can be as low as 4 percent or as much as 30 percent, or even higher) and takes a valuable item as collateral. If the person doesn't pay up within an agreed-upon time frame, the pawnshop can sell the guitar, Rolex watch, television, or whatever the pawned item was. While pawnshops prefer to give loans, because that's where the big bucks are, it's possible they'll want to buy your computer, signed baseball card collection, or vintage jewelry outright. If you don't have any other takers, a pawnshop could be worth checking out.

THINK ABOUT WHO YOU KNOW

Personal contacts are a great market for selling some high-ticket items. When I realized I had an old camera, flash, lens, and camera bag to sell, I remembered I knew someone who had expressed interest in it months before. I ended up selling it to her at a good price. I quickly got rid of the items (time = value!), my friend was happy, I was happy, and because I sold it slightly undervalue, my business was able to take the sale as a loss at tax time.

A Photographer's Secrets to Amazing Online Listings

Again, time is important, so I'm not suggesting you spend hours taking photos of the stuff you want to sell online, but if you keep the following tips in mind when taking pictures, your listings will look good and be more likely to bring in cash. Our society is obsessed with visuals; people pay for pretty. Also, know that these suggestions also work for your phone's camera. Nothing fancy is needed to create an attractive online listing.

Find a space by a large window (or take the photos outside). Look for a simple, nondistracting background and remove any clutter that's nearby. The stack of old newspapers that need to be put in the recycling bin probably won't help highlight your designer handbag's loveliest features. If a bright window is making too much of a contrast between the of light and dark areas on your item, have a friend hold up a large piece of white paper or poster board on the shadow side of the item to reflect light into the dark spots.

Make sure your item is wearing its "Sunday best." In other words, clean it up, fluff it up, and de-scuff it. You don't want it looking dirty or worn out in the pictures. Also, consider styling options. If you're trying to sell a really nice dress, ask your best-looking friend to put it on for a photo and shoot her from the front, side, and back. If you're selling a set of plates, think about ever so casually tucking a textured piece of fabric off to the side so that it's peeking into the corner of the frame, looking like a classy table linen.

Include detail and overview shots. Take photographs of anything that's broken or stained so you can make buyers aware of flaws and unique features. Giving a person as much info about the item upfront reduces the chances of minds getting changed when they see it in person, saving everyone the time and bother of having to deal with returns, refunds, or canceled deals.

If you're using your phone for the pictures, consider sprucing them up with a free photo-editing app. My favorite photo app is VSCO.

Being Minimalist Doesn't Mean Having Nothing

My big purge immediately had a positive impact on my life. I had less stuff to clean, and I knew exactly where absolutely everything was. I was so excited that I decided to take it a step further (because go big or go home, right?) and take on the Minimalist Challenge. Minimalism isn't about saying good-bye to all your worldly possessions and living in a stark white room with nothing but a bed, one strategically placed houseplant, and a white whisper-thin curtain blowing peacefully in a light breeze. While getting rid of everything you own in one swoop is certainly an efficient approach to minimizing your belongings, there's another, slightly slower way to incorporate minimalism into your life. You can make the conscious decision, over and over, to fill your life with only positive things, people, technologies, and responsibilities. You want to rethink, and potentially get rid of, all the things that are weighing you down. You're not limited to keeping a particular number of things or to eliminating a certain amount.

If you want to take on the Minimalist Challenge, as I did, check out the 30-Day Minimalism Game on the Minimalists' website, www.TheMinimalists.com/game. You'll find a friend to "compete" with and attempt to spend thirty days getting rid of stuff. On day one, you toss *one* thing; on day two, *two* things; all the way up to thirty things by day thirty. Whoever can keep the game going the longest wins. If you make it to day thirty, you'll have gotten rid of 465 things!

$ Let's Do This!

- ❑ Designate five areas for items: sell, trash, or donate, recycle, and give away.
- ❑ Collect all the quick, no-brainer items you can easily get rid of.
- ❑ Go through every single area of each room in your house and gather things to get rid of. Place them in the proper sell/trash/donate/recycle/give away area.
- ❑ Consider which of the things to be sold are high-ticket items. They are the ones you will put the most effort into selling.
- ❑ Decide where to sell the high-ticket items: Craigslist or Instagram, personal contacts, pawnshops.
- ❑ Consolidate your efforts and decide how you can quickly sell the bulk of your items.

SOMETIMES YOU HAVE TO DO WHAT'S BEST FOR YOU, NOT WHAT'S BEST FOR EVERYONE ELSE.

CHAPTER 11

The Social Side of the Spending Fast

I remember exactly how it feels. You're committed to your Spending Fast and getting closer to reaching your goal of getting out of debt. You've cut back on expenses, gone without (sacrifice for the win!), and found ways to make more money. It's all going really well and you're benefiting from the many positive changes you've made. Then along comes a baby shower, your best friend's wedding, or a regular night out with friends. Before you know it, you're pulling out that credit card and charging plane tickets, a blender, a giant stuffed animal for your friend's baby, or a really expensive dinner that later you're not sure was worth it.

I get it. The social side of the Spending Fast is tough to navigate. As I've said before, our money problems aren't just about not having enough money; they stem from every single choice we make. And many of those choices are the result of feeling like we have to keep up with others or being afraid to say no. Managing the social side of the Spending Fast takes tenacity—and I'm hoping that some of the things I've learned and share in this chapter will make following your Spending Fast a little bit easier.

You're Never Alone

No one really does a Spending Fast alone. Sure, it's your debt and your mistakes, and you're the only one who can turn the situation around. However, committing to a

Spending Fast definitely affects the people you are closest to. Your friends and family influence how you spend money, and your newfound choice to *not* spend is definitely going to create waves.

As I mentioned, my breakdown moment happened shortly after my wedding. I was feeling crushed by debt and my lack of control over it. It's one thing to cease spending when it affects only you, but when you've just made a commitment to spend the rest of your life with another person, you're definitely dragging that person into your Spending Fast. Aaron hated the idea of the Spending Fast in the beginning (and it didn't help that I committed to it without telling him first). Aaron has never had a problem with overspending, so I was worried that if we discussed it all prior to me starting, he'd think the Spending Fast was too extreme and would try to talk me out of it. Even though we'd been married for over seven months, we weren't sharing a bank account. Naively, I thought the Spending Fast would be this process that I went through alone. I figured our relationship would go on as normal, and then, *Bam! Hurray!* I'd be out of debt. I was very wrong.

Spouses, Significant Others, and Family Members Have Needs Too

My committing to the Spending Fast, while ultimately the right decision, was very difficult for our relationship. There were challenges I didn't anticipate, and it would have been better if I had discussed some of this stuff with Aaron up front *before* I dove in. Aaron admits that he had a "fearful concern" when I told him I was doing the Fast. He knows that I tend to be an all-or-nothing kind of person, and he could see that going cold turkey with spending was likely to stress our new marriage. In the beginning, until I really figured things out, Aaron ended up paying for certain purchases because I wouldn't or didn't want to. At one point he was actually worried that because he was picking up the slack, he'd end up in debt while I would be out of it. I also overstepped bounds by mooching. Aaron told me straight up that the mooching wasn't cool, so I did my best to avoid it. I occasionally asked for bites of things, and Aaron would tell me, "I don't do bites." If he wanted to get take-out, I'd suggest a "you buy, I'll fly" deal (if he paid for the food, I'd go pick it up) to feel as if I was earning my share. But it wasn't enough. I compromised by giving myself a small monthly allowance of $30 to spend on or with Aaron.

I know I've talked about not letting yourself come up with "new" Needs, but I felt there was no point in doing the Spending Fast if I was going to be divorced in the end. Even though it was hard for me to take $30 away from the money I'd earmarked for putting toward my debt, having a little bit of my own spending money took some of the stress off our relationship. I hate that the Spending Fast made our marriage rocky in the beginning, but Aaron agrees with me now that this was coming from a good place. I knew that if I could do the Spending Fast and get out of debt, we'd have a more stable foundation for our future.

Now that we have a child, a successful wedding photography business, and a mortgage, it's more important than ever that I figured out my finances as early as I did. I knew I'd made some really positive, lasting changes when Aaron finally agreed to share a bank account with me. I'll always be grateful to my naturally inclined Saver of a husband for sticking with me. It probably wasn't fun for him to watch his wife dye her clothes on the kitchen stove and eat unusual concoctions made from random canned food for dinner. Looking back, I can see there were definitely a few things I could have done to make the Spending Fast less stressful on Aaron and on our relationship.

If We'd Known, We Would Have . . .

Before you take on the challenge of your own Spending Fast, talk with the people in your life about how to deal with any tension the Fast might cause in your relationships. How will you handle the ways it will affect your daily life?

> **Hash out specifics.** What exactly does the Spending Fast mean for your partner? If you can help it, don't wait until after you've started the Fast to figure out how it's all going to work.

> **Discuss the fine line between "asking" and "mooching."** You don't want to be tit for tat about every purchase, but it's true that you can't expect someone to "treat" you forever without expecting something in return.

Make sure you determine your Needs as a couple. If necessary, make a list of the Needs you share as a couple. If you're both paying for certain expenses, you can't suddenly decide they're moving to the Wants list without consulting with the other person. You'll have to decide together what stays and goes, and how you'll deal with any differences of opinion.

CONTROL YOUR MOOCHING

Since Aaron was front and center for all my mooching, I asked him to share his thoughts on this subject: "Mooching is a powder keg waiting to explode. A big part of any Spending Fast is personal sacrifice. You may want an ice cream cone, but just because your spouse/boyfriend/girlfriend/best friend/family member stopped for one, it doesn't mean he or she is willing to buy you one as well. Deal with the fact that you will be hearing no, accept it with a smile, and move on. Remember, you're the one who voluntarily decided to do the Spending Fast."

When You're Not on the Same Page

I often hear from readers that they just aren't on the same page with their spouses or significant others about money. It seems as though one person falls into the Spender category while the other one is the Saver. This is all relative, of course, because in past relationships I was the Saver, whereas now, compared to Aaron, I'm the Spender. In *The Psychological Science of Money,* Erik Bijleveld and Henk Aarts explain that a person's "pain of paying" or their spending style can definitely cause conflict in relationships. If that's not enough, they also say that people tend to marry someone who has a totally different style from their own. Spendthrifts attract tightwads and vice versa. The difference between those spending styles eventually results in conflict, aka big-ass fights over money.

One woman wrote to me because she wanted to do the Spending Fast to deal with the debt she and her husband had accumulated together, but he wasn't into it. She said no matter how much they talked and planned, and as much as he would seem to be on board while they were doing the talking and planning, when it came down to it, he wouldn't agree to change his behavior. This isn't unusual, and don't feel bad if your partner isn't sold on the idea of the Fast from the beginning. Give yourself a pat on the back for continuing to do what *you* can do to be financially responsible.

That said, if I've learned anything from the drama of my personal Spending Fast relationship situation, it's that keeping the lines of communication open is crucial when it comes to the topic of money. Even if those lines aren't always the most pleasant. There's no question that it's easy to get resentful, especially if one person in the partnership wants to get out of debt and the other couldn't care less. While you're trying to get on the same page, the debt is just getting bigger and bigger. If your partner has previously handled the finances, discuss the option of your taking over, but in a "let me take that burden off your back" kind of way.

Think about how you can find common ground with your loved one about the way you handle money as a couple. There's no shame in going to marriage counseling. In fact, there are some counselors who actually specialize in financial issues and helping couples develop a healthier relationship with money. Money issues are a huge problem for many couples, and seeking professional help may be just what you need. I'd also recommend taking a look at *Smart Couples Finish Rich: 9 Steps to Creating a Rich Future for You and Your Partner* by David Bach—he's got good things to say on the subject.

Expensive Social Situations for Every Stage of Life: How to Deal

While the Spending Fast presented a particular challenge for me in my role as half of a newly married couple, there are countless social scenarios that can drain your wallet, whether you have a partner or not. While it's tough to say no to yourself (you haven't bought a new top in months, or you've been dying to see that movie!), that's a battle you're waging with *yourself*, which in some ways is easier than arguing with someone else. How should you handle turning down invitations to the countless other activities and life events that require money be spent?

It's difficult to get over this hurdle, but the most important step is to try to get to the point where you stop caring about what people think. It takes maturity and confidence not to care if people think you're a miser. And again, hopefully by now you've figured out that you simply don't need people in your life who are overly concerned with the cost and brand of your clothes, electronics, car, how often you go out, where you go on vacation, and so on. I was once told by a wise woman, "What other people think about you is none of your business. You do you." The same insightful woman told me, "When someone gives you a hard time about something, it's usually because their own insecurities are bubbling up, and they don't like what they see. Don't take things personally—99.9 percent of the time it has nothing to do with you and everything to do with what they're struggling with internally." Granted, worrying less won't happen overnight, especially if you've spent your whole life fretting over other people's opinions of you. But trust me, life (and all its social situations) gets easier when you're proud and confident about your choices.

Another way to manage expensive life events is to get creative and find less expensive alternatives.

You Can Still Give Awesome Gifts

Many of my readers have expressed concern about how they will be able to give gifts to celebrate major life milestones such as weddings, bridal and baby showers, and new babies while on the Spending Fast. It's one thing to cut back on birthday and holiday gifts (do your adult friends really need more lotion or yet another scented candle?), but it feels really crummy to hold off on a big-occasion gift because of your Fast. I get it—someone close to you has just celebrated a major life event and you don't want to give them the shaft because of your financial mess. What can you do to honor your friend that won't mess up your Spending Fast?

Feed Your Friends

How would you feel if once a month a friend arrived at your door with a lovingly prepared meal or a basket of muffins? If you can't afford to buy a wedding gift, offer to feed your friends instead. Life is busy and many people don't have time to prepare home-cooked meals! Giving a meal or pan of treats is a wonderful way to celebrate a friend's new marriage, and any parent will tell you that not having to cook for the first weeks of a baby's life because other people did the work for them is basically the best gift ever. If you're a good cook, plan a night where you drop off a meal. You could do this once, a few times, or if you're really generous, once a month for an entire year. If you're more of a baker, drop off muffins or cookies. If your friend lives far away, pack up and send a month's supply of homemade granola. If cooking isn't your thing, find a good budget-friendly wine and leave a bottle on their porch the first Friday of every month (safely tucked out of view of passersby, of course). Get creative. If someone was going to bring you food, treats, or wine, what would make you happiest? What would make *your* eyes light up?

Use Your Skills to Make a Gift

Cooking or baking isn't everyone's thing. Think about what skills you have that could be used to create a memorable gift. If you're crafty, make a frame for your friends' favorite wedding photo or an ornament for their first Christmas together. Since I'm a photographer, I've given the gift of family portrait sessions, and I've offered to take pictures at an important milestone, such as a baby's first birthday. It's really easy to get stuck thinking that something has to be tangible to count as a gift, but it doesn't have to be. Are you an amazing landscaper? Offer to help a couple who've just bought a house to create a beautiful garden. If you're a writer, help family or friends celebrating a milestone anniversary by documenting the story of how they met. If you're great with kids, offer to babysit so their parents can have a date night. When you're thoughtful and consider unconventional options—such as sharing your talents as a gift—the recipient will likely be more appreciative than you think, and will welcome the unconventional present.

House Sit, Cat Sit, Plant Sit: Sit All the Things

Not having to worry about little details such as your cat starving or your prize orchids dying is a gift in itself. Offer to take care of pet needs, house sitting (and collecting mail and the paper), watering plants, and so on so that when your friends take a vacation or travel for work, these details are covered.

Can You Return Something?

As you now know, I'm not shy about returning stuff. Think about recent purchases that you may be able to return in order to get a little extra cash for a wedding or baby gift. If you can get only a store credit, that's fine—be sure to ask for it in the form of a gift card. Speaking of . . .

Any Random Gift Cards?

If you received a gift card for the holidays or a birthday that happens to be appropriate for your friend who is celebrating, pass it along. Newlyweds and new parents tend to make a lot of purchases as they navigate the new territory of marriage and parenthood. I know from personal experience that gift cards are always very appreciated.

Barter for Someone Else's Skills

So let's say your friends who got married *love* wine, and your next-door neighbor just so happens to be a sommelier at a local restaurant. Think about what skills you have (or tasks you could offer up) that you can use to barter with your wine expert neighbor. Maybe she needs her dog walked every evening? Offer to take over dog-walking services for a month (or more) in exchange for her presiding over a small wine tasting at the home of your newly married oenophile friends.

There are a million ways this kind of bartering can work. When you utilize your exclusive blend of talents and connections, you just may be able to give your friends their favorite gift of all time without even spending a dime.

A Word on Random Gifts

When you work in an office, it seems as if someone is always having a baby, getting married, having a birthday, or retiring—because they are. E-mails get sent out: "Let's all chip in $10 for Ryan's birthday cake and present!" No doubt you want to be a nice coworker, but dropping your hard-earned cash on random celebrations at the office for people you barely know can be painful. The holidays are tricky too—it seems as if there are suddenly lots of people in your life you have to get gifts for to show your appreciation. You don't want to skip your boss, mentor, babysitter, super-helpful neighbor, kid's teacher, or professor. Instead, remember that celebrating a coworker's retirement or showing appreciation to a boss doesn't have to mean spending money. It's easy to underestimate the power of a well-written, heartfelt letter. It's rare that we're told how we're appreciated or how we positively influence someone else's life. Your boss is probably already getting a lot of Starbucks gift cards; a good, heartfelt letter might end up being the stand-out gift.

$60 Salad Syndrome

We've all been there. You're at dinner with friends, hanging out or maybe celebrating someone's birthday. You're committed to your Spending Fast, so you graciously skip the appetizers, wine, dessert—and even the entrée. You order a modest salad for yourself (the least expensive thing on the menu, *thank you very much*) and decide to enjoy the company of your friends rather than an expensive meal. You've chosen to go without, which is commendable. You cried inside a little while everyone was going on and on about the tiramisu and chocolate cake, but you made it through.

Then the bill comes. It's *massive*. The kind of bill that you'll go home and text your sister about. "You'll never believe how much the bill for dinner was!" While you were pretending to be full after your meager mesclun salad with the sliver of goat cheese, your friends had elaborate entrées and multiple cocktails. To your further dismay, whoever grabbed the bill announces, "Hey, guys! Let's just make it easy and split it equally! Let's see . . . that makes it $60 per person." Your eyes involuntarily bulge, you go slack-jawed, and your tongue rolls out as if you're in a cartoon and a large anvil just fell off an overhanging cliff onto you. You want to die. No way do you want to pay $60 for a salad fit for a bunny.

But what do you do? Many of us have caved, too embarrassed to point out we didn't order as much as everyone else *on purpose,* or because we're afraid of looking cheap. We hesitantly hand over a credit card, seething inside, only to go home and eat a piece of toast and a limp celery stick from the veggie drawer. How do you avoid $60 Salad Syndrome? There are a few ways to handle it, as I'll explain below. Choose whichever one works for you, but know that you should never fork over money you don't have for other people's extravagant dinners. How do you handle a split check with grace?

Tactic One: Cash + A Separate Check

Get cash before the dinner and make sure you have a variety of denominations so that you won't have to ask for change. When it's time to place your order, tell the server that you'd like a separate check. If your server isn't standing right next to you when you place your order, and you don't want to shout, "And oh, I want a separate check," politely indicate that you'd like to speak with him when he's done taking orders. Or excuse yourself to go to wash your hands, find your server along the way, and tell her you didn't get a chance to mention that you need a separate check. When *your* check arrives, pull out the cash *for your meal only.* Obviously, this tactic would work when paying with a debit card too, but paying with cash is more discreet and doesn't involve another step in the transaction at the end of dinner.

Tactic Two: Give What You Owe to the Person with the Check

It's perfectly acceptable to say, "I had a salad and a pop; here's what I owe." That's polite, truthful, and you're not making a big deal about it. Hand your money to the person at the table who grabbed the check and decided it was being divided by the number of people at the table, instead of by who ordered what. The thing is, at a big dinner, it's entirely possible that no one even noticed you had only one small thing. Often checks are divided based on the assumption that everyone is drinking a lot and ordering multiple courses. Keeping calm is always a good tactic to take when negotiating the tricky situation of a large dinner bill. Just remember to leave enough to cover tax and the tip. While I totally support your paying for just the stuff you ordered, it's uncool to stick your friends with the all the tax and the entire tip.

If it's really hard for you to feel comfortable jumping in and pointing out you had only a salad, ask a friend to help. We all have one of those boisterous, outspoken friends. Ask that person in advance to speak up for you and your tiny, cheap meal when someone announces the bill is being split in a way that works against you.

Tactic Three: Dinner or Dessert

If you want to join the party, but don't want to deal with the check awkwardness, make a point of joining your friends for drinks before dinner or just for dessert. The bonus to doing drinks is that you can keep it ultra-cheap by ordering a sparkling water. When they head toward their table to sit down for dinner, say you've got to go but it was great to seeing everyone, yadda yadda. You'll have acknowledged your friend's special occasion without compromising your Spending Fast.

To meet up with the party after the meal, have a friend text you to let you know when dessert time is approaching. Showing up at the end of the meal and ordering dessert is a great way to join in the fun, but it's totally obvious you weren't there for the entire meal. No one is going to try to get $60 out of you for a bite of cake.

We've all been in a situation where we end up paying for way more than we should. Don't feel embarrassed to ask for a separate check or speak up for yourself about how much you really owe. When it comes down to it, you have to be your own advocate. The reality is, no one should begrudge your paying the appropriate amount for what you ate.

Out-of-the-Box Group Outings

It's often hard to think of something fun to do with friends that doesn't involve going to a restaurant or bar. It's fun to have people over, but it's not going to be good for your Spending Fast if you're forking over money every other week for cheese platters. Come up with creative ways to hang out with your friends that won't involve dropping loads of money. There's always that moment when you're making plans and someone says, "Well, what should we do?" Be ready to seize that moment and respond with a few free or low-cost suggestions.

Eating and Drinking

Going to restaurants is fun. Meeting friends out is also fun. If drinking beer and eating is what you found yourself spending money on pre–Spending Fast, think about how you can re-create that experience at home. Consider inviting your friends over to share classic potluck dinners. If you want to make them extra fun, have themes. Maybe you'll do seventies casseroles one month and BBQ the next. Since the Spending Fast always requires you to save more and dig deeper, ask your friends to bring whatever's gotta go from their refrigerators. One person may have extra greens, another some extra chicken breasts and pasta. Someone might show up with a couple of apples and some walnuts. Consider it a challenge to take everyone's food and turn it into a feast. Not only will you have fun with friends, you'll make sure every last bit of food in your house is eaten.

Brunch is another major money suck. It's very eye-opening to see how cheap it is to make pancakes and mimosas at home. Tell your inner Spender to get outta here, and invite your friends to your place for brunch instead of meeting at a restaurant. Not only will you save tons of money, you won't waste half of your Sunday waiting for a table.

Don't Let Kids Drain You Financially

Every parent knows that kids can cost a fortune. There's the obvious stuff, such as feeding and clothing them—and day care is a colossal expense. Then there are the less obvious costs that pop up and add to your spending. As kids get older, there are loads of activities that they understandably want to participate in. But what can you do when you're on a Spending Fast and your kid is really into playing soccer? Is it fair to pull your kid off the soccer team and have him or her miss out on all the fun and other benefits? With some careful planning and imagination, there are some ways to keep your kids involved in activities without spending the $100 to $200 it costs to participate in organized sports.

Band Together

The truth is, you're probably not the only parent looking to save money. You don't have to go around town announcing you're on a Spending Fast, but it's easy enough to suggest to others that you're looking for alternatives to the expensive tennis lessons your kid is interested in. Think about how you can provide something similar to the big-bucks experience but at a much-reduced cost. If your child is into soccer, talk to some other soccer parents and see if any of them might be into creating a low-frills soccer club with you. Investigate what soccer skills training you can reasonably re-create, and see who else you can recruit from your community. Maybe each week the kids can meet at a park and adults who've signed up for different time slots will practice and play with the kids. Maybe rotate playing in one another's backyards. If your little soccer syndicate grew to include enough children, you'd probably be able to arrange for one team of kids to play games against another. If one parent volunteers to "coach," what could you do for that person to make it worth the time? What skills do you have that they don't? Maybe they suck at baking (and you're amazing at it) and they need a birthday cake for their kid next month. Be creative and see how you can work with other members of your community to help one another out.

Barter

Does the woman down the street play the piano? Maybe she'll give your children lessons in exchange for your help with the website for her business. I had a positive bartering experience during my Spending Fast. I desperately needed to get my hair done but wasn't going to spend the money on myself. I found a stylist who needed photographs taken. She did my hair, I did her photographs, and it was a perfect exchange.

Maybe you can help a neighbor by walking her kid to school with yours, and in exchange she'll take yours so you can have a date night from time to time. Bartering is good both for the bank account and for community spirit.

Borrow

Borrowing is a great way to save money when it comes to kids especially—but just about any general house stuff you might need for a short period of time can be borrowed. Remember begging your parents to get you that guitar, trampoline, Ping-Pong table, or whatever whimsical, expensive thing you had to have when you were twelve? And how after just a few Ping-Pong tournaments with friends, you were over it? If there's something you're thinking about getting and a neighbor already has one, ask if you can try theirs. If your child wants to try ice skating, see who in the 'hood has skates in their size. If you need some random tool for a home repair that you're probably never going to use again, *borrow* one. You'll also need to return borrowed items promptly so that you maintain a reputation as a good borrower, and obviously, if you don't like the idea of people borrowing *your* things in return, this solution probably isn't a great option for you.

$ Let's Do This!

❑ If you're partnered, talk with your partner about your long-term financial goals. Having no debt is an amazing foundation to build a life on.

❑ Talk about how the Spending Fast will likely affect your day-to-day life, and what you think that might look like.

❑ Discuss which parts of the Spending Fast you think will be the easiest and the most difficult, and how you will approach the tough times.

❑ Think about the social situations you're most worried about and decide on a plan of action. This can keep you from making a bad decision out of panic.

❑ Get creative with your kid-related spending.

CHAPTER 12

Good-bye, Spending Fast;
Hello, Spending Diet!

You may have fasted for one super-intense month, or maybe you stuck it out for a full year. Whatever time frame you chose, it's a big deal when your Fast finally comes to an end. I know what that feels like, and I'm here to tell you that you've done an amazing thing for yourself! You're now in a great position to start managing your money in a healthy new way. If you're anything like I was, you're really surprised it's over, and you're not sure what to do next. Let's start with this—congratulations! You did it! Your Spending Fast is *over*. You sacrificed, you said no more times than you can count, and you ate some really weird stuff along the way. You definitely need to take a moment to celebrate this amazing achievement.

I still remember how it felt to write about the end of my Spending Fast on my blog. I was a giant walking cliché. My shoulders felt looser, I had a huge smile on my face, and all I could think was, *I really frickin' did it!* I couldn't believe I'd made such a giant dent in my debt. Originally I was just hoping to pay off my $6,000 in credit card debt, but my progress was going so well that I stuck to the Fast, wiped out $12,175.45 of my other debt as well (for a total of $18,175.45 paid), and had only $5,429.65 left to pay on my student loan. I had proven to myself that I could do hard things, and I was confident I'd be able to pay off my remaining debt before too long.

After the Spending Fast ended I took a couple of days off from Needs-Only spending, which resulted in my immediately dropping $150 on a pair of boots. It was then that I realized I needed to follow up my Spending Fast with a Spending Diet. A Spending Diet is similar to a Spending Fast but takes a slightly different approach to Wants: You're allowed to have them, at least to a certain budgeted extent. I didn't want to slip back into my old habits, but I was aware that the intensity of the Fast wasn't sustainable. I was really proud that I went an entire year spending money on Needs Only, and even though I was still technically in debt, I was determined to figure out a way to continue all this hard work without Fasting. I needed to figure out some sort of maintenance plan to keep me in a good place—which ideally meant not spending money on random stuff while I paid off the rest of my debt, and when that was over my focus would turn to saving!

One thing I learned quickly—and I admit it was a bit surprising—is that the Spending Diet was harder than I expected. Some spending decisions were no longer black and white, and there were fewer simple choices such as "The Eco Pass is on my Needs list, so I can buy it!" Before we dive into the next challenging stage of the Debt Removal process, let me take a second to suggest you celebrate your awesomeness with a rowdy "Hell yeah!" Go to the mirror right this minute and repeat after me: "I'm unstoppable! I'm killing this debt as I knew I would!" Just take a second to look at yourself being straight up amazing.

> *Hey, Anna, I just wanted to let you know that after two years and $70,000 in student loans, my husband and I will be debt-free at the end of the month. We owe a debt of gratitude to you and others in the financial community for the practical resources and encouragement along our journey.* —Sydney

> *So far I have paid off one small credit card, but this is a great feeling for me. Soon I will knock out the next small one, then on to the bigger ones.* —Amanda

> *My husband and I recently paid off all our debt—a little over $52,000 in two years. It feels great to be debt-free! It was so hard but so worth it.* —Tara

From last February until now we've paid off approximately $10,000 worth of debt between the two of us, we've saved $26,000, and we've contributed significant amounts to our retirement funds.

—Lisa

My financial struggles seem so much more manageable. By taking part in the Spending Fast, I was able to pay off $3,000 in credit card debt in just over six months without missing any other bill payments. Oh, did I mention that I only make $11 an hour at my full-time job?

—Alex

Celebrate: For Free

I'm sure when I say, "Celebrate your goals!" you're thinking, *Yeahhhh, and how do you expect that to happen when I can't spend money?* I promise, I do still remember how it hurts to have to turn down fun plans with friends. Remember, celebrations do not have to mean spending a ton of money (or any, for that matter). The important part about celebrating the completion of your Spending Fast is that you recognize your achievements in a way that's meaningful to you. In true Spending Fast fashion, I've thought of a few ways you can celebrate cost-free. Hopefully, you're also able to focus on how good it feels in and of itself to no longer be living in a financial shitstorm. It's time now to learn to celebrate your accomplishments while not simultaneously derailing everything you've done.

It's really easy to convince yourself to spend money because you "deserve it." And while you do in fact deserve a reward for meeting a goal, requiring an actual material item every time you accomplish a feat is not a good philosophy or habit to get into. Of course there are times in life when something amazing happens and a bottle of champagne or a dinner out feels like the right way to celebrate. And that's okay. You'll remember that there was a time when your old way of thinking was: *My friend moved into a new apartment! Let's go shopping!* Trouble comes when celebrating an achievement or life event becomes a veiled excuse to buy yourself something. The Spending Diet is the perfect time to learn to celebrate yourself and your accomplishments with experiences and things that don't cost money.

You Deserve It! Ways to Celebrate for Free (or Nearly Free)

Sleep in.

Give yourself a home mani-pedi.

Take a bubble bath.

Listen to your guilty pleasure music. Bust out your Taylor Swift and Mariah Carey CDs and put "Right Here Waiting" on repeat.

Devote an evening to Netflix viewing.

Indulge in the glory of your awesomeness for ten minutes. Truly appreciate that you've accomplished your goal.

Lose yourself in an Instagram black hole.

Get a copy of Us Weekly from the grocery store line, lie down on the couch, and read every single juicy page.

Make your favorite cookies or a batch of brownies.

Log some guilt-free Pinterest time. You know what I mean.

Lay in the grass in the park.

Get on the couch with a book and don't get up until you're finished.

Ignore housework and chores for a day and enjoy your favorite hobby.

Go to the library and grab every book or magazine that interests you.

Get yourself a damn Filet-O-Fish (my mom's go-to treat).

Pop your earbuds in and walk around your neighborhood binge-listening to your favorite podcasts.

Wake up early, brew coffee or tea, and watch the sun rise.

If your gym has a sauna or steam room—go use it.

Use some of your paid time off from work and spend the day any way you want.

Stay in your PJs all day.

Eat cake for breakfast.

It's a Lot Like Losing Those Last Few Pounds

Have you ever had a moment where you realize your jeans are too tight and you gotta drop a few pounds so your jeans will fit better? Maybe your high school reunion is coming up and you want to look and feel your best when you see your old friends. Whatever your reason, you realize you have to cut back. You stop making pie every week. You convince yourself you're happy with smaller portions. You spend time sweating at the gym when you could be at home watching a movie.

At first the extra work isn't fun—it's a total drag. But then those numbers on the scale start going down, and before you know it those jeans you desperately wanted to fit into are getting loose! You feel healthier and stronger. People notice your glow and comment on how you seem more confident.

It's entirely possible to emit the same outward glow from knowing you have a healthier bank balance. Before the Spending Fast, I was stressed and worried all the time, and it showed. Post-Fast, happiness, contentment, and a proud new feeling of accomplishment permeated everything I did.

But what if I forgot about the path I'd taken to get there? If the night of your class reunion you down three cocktails chock-full of calories and have fourths on dessert, you're not going to feel so great. If you follow up the next day with a breakfast fit for a lumberjack and decide you *deserve* a family-sized package of Pepperidge Farm cookies, those jeans may once again not fit.

It's probably pretty obvious that the same logic applies to the Spending Diet. You've made it through the Spending Fast, but can you use what you've learned about yourself to safely navigate your way in the next stage? There are temptations everywhere, and you don't have the same protections you had just a short while ago. That's why it's crucial to take the Spending Diet as seriously as you did your Spending Fast if you want to continue to chip away at debt and start to get money into a savings account.

I Was Found, Then I Was Lost

I'm going to be perfectly honest with you. At first I sucked at the Spending Diet. My "I did it" feeling of accomplishment soon morphed into an "OMG. Am I going to end up right back where is started?" feeling of dread. It turns out that the structure of the Spending Fast kept me more on track than I ever realized. I didn't have to think very much about purchases at all. Things were cut-and-dry. If something was on the Wants side, it was easy to turn it down. On the Spending Diet, I found it very difficult to navigate my Wants without worrying that I was slipping (quickly) back into my old autopilot spending ways. Post-Fast, I bought some pants that I genuinely needed. After a year of wearing the same clothes over and over, some of them had become threadbare. I got a pair of black work pants for a ridiculously low price and I still felt guilty. I simply wasn't used to spending. I remember at that time I was also obsessing over a pair of boots that I just had to have. I had been ogling them online during the last six months of my Spending Fast. They were The Most Perfect Boots Ever, and I ordered them six seconds after the Fast ended. I anxiously awaited their arrival, and when they finally came I ripped the package open and tried them on right there in the entryway of my home. I took two steps and noticed my perfect boots were strangely noisy. *What's that noise? No way. It couldn't be the boots . . . could it? It was.* I returned them the next day.

It turns out I enjoyed those boots only during the six months I spent dreaming about how great they would be. Once I actually owned them, the magic had faded.

I'm not alone in this. As mentioned earlier in the book, studies show that wanting things makes us happier than actually having them. Marsha Richins from the University of Missouri evaluated the emotional state of "materialists" (people who are markedly more concerned with material things than with spiritual, intellectual, or cultural values) before and after making an important purchase. It turns out that the materialists felt strong positive emotions—joy, excitement, optimism, and even peacefulness—just thinking about buying something, even if they weren't going to buy it until the next week or the next year. What happened after the purchase was made? There was a "hedonic decline." Those happy feelings? Gone. For many people, the anticipation of acquiring something is more enjoyable than actually getting it.

Unsure of how to navigate my desire for things with my new habits, I decided to give myself $100 a month to spend on items that weren't on my Needs list. I flew through that money *really* fast. It was so easy to spend it *all*. I didn't have any scientific reason for choosing $100. It seemed like a reasonable amount, and I knew I had to start somewhere.

Time to Regroup

Not long after the boot disappointment, I realized I had to reflect on why I was able to keep my behavior in check during the Spending Fast, but was struggling to keep it together on the Spending Diet. I knew I couldn't go back to my old ways—the changes I made needed to be forever if I didn't want to rack up my credit card debt again. So why was it so hard to make good financial choices without the structure of the Fast? After some serious reflection, I realized that there were a few things I learned about myself on the Fast that I still needed to address. As I said before, it was becoming clear that I had a lot more to learn; the Fast didn't magically cure all of my issues with money. The key to being successful on a Spending Diet was making sure I dealt with these particular issues.

I Have Triggers

The post-Fast boot obsession made it clear that I have some triggers I have to be on the lookout for. My pining over a pair of boots and convincing myself that I *needed* them is typical behavior for me. As you may remember from the incident with the coat from J. Crew (the one I had to have even though it was expensive and made me look like I was wearing a grocery bag), I can easily convince myself that a Want is a Need. I let myself get so worked up about a particular item that the situation quickly morphs from "Last year's coat is still really cute and in good shape. Great! I won't need a new coat for a year or two" to "I need this coat. My life depends on my getting this coat." I was repeating the same cycle with the boots. A want quickly became a need, which is how I got into financial trouble in the first place. I needed to figure out how to keep my Wants and Needs in check.

I Am Just an All-Out Kind of Girl

Another important thing I learned about myself on the Spending Fast is that I'm really an all-or-nothing kind of person. I started noticing this trend coming up in all areas of my life. For example: If I like a food, I'll eat it for every meal for a month straight. If I decide to start working out, I won't just go for a few jogs here and there. Nope. I figure, *Might as well train for a fitness competition!* And when I get a couple of consecutive days of journaling under my belt, I think, *Might as well write my memoir while I'm at it.* Moderation is clearly not my thing.

This is undoubtedly why the black-and-white nature of the Spending Fast worked so well for me, but it's also the reason I could so easily get in trouble again. I had to learn how to find a middle ground with some of my purchases. For example, I love making crafts. I'm good at it, and it's something I really enjoy doing. After the Fast I wanted to make a new craft that required some felt. I noticed that it was very difficult for me to buy only the two pieces of felt the craft called for. I wanted to go all out and buy *tons* of felt. I basically wanted to get enough so that I could open up my very own felt store. I needed to learn how to make regular purchases without going overboard.

I Need to Regularly Reassess My Needs and How Much They Cost

One really positive trait I learned about myself during the Fast was that I'm really good at knocking down the costs of my Needs. I reflected on how I was able to completely eliminate some of my Needs, and others I was able to acquire much cheaper. It's a mistake to think your Wants and Needs List is set in stone—that you make the list once, figure out how to do some of the stuff more cheaply right away, and then forget about the list. Since the Spending Fast I've continued to save money by re-evaluating everything on my Needs list. For example, remember how I got my gym membership knocked down by $15 per month? I had assumed that my YMCA rate was the best deal in town, but it wasn't. By looking around further I learned that a 24-Hour Fitness nearby was cheaper. I was really surprised and glad that I found the savings. I was also buying nongrocery items at the Family Dollar, since I had always heard that you should never buy things like shampoo at the grocery store. I assumed I was getting the cheapest price at the Family Dollar (I mean, come on, it's the Family Dollar). Turns out I was wrong again. Shampoo and other personal care products were actually cheaper at the grocery store. I was also able to negotiate a better deal on our cell phone plans. By taking the time to sit down and reevaluate the costs of our Needs, I was able to save myself a chunk of money each month.

Taking It Further, Again

Once I took the time to reflect on my behavior during the Spending Fast, I felt as if I was more in control. I knew that a budget would never work for me: I'm not the kind of person who likes to deal with categories and very defined dollar amounts. I knew that I had to have faith that my newfound healthy spending habits were here to stay, but taking the time to note my strengths and weaknesses with money really helped. Reflecting on the reasons that made the Fast work for me really gave me the confidence I needed to move forward and get comfortable with the idea of spending money in a normal way.

What Did You Learn?

My rocky start with the Spending Diet made me realize how important it is to take a close look at what you learned during the Fast. While everyone's issues with money are different, it's important to acknowledge and deal with those issues during the next stage of the process. While I love hearing that the Spending Fast got people out of debt, I also enjoy hearing about what people learned about themselves while they were undergoing the Fast. I believe it's that extra bit of self-awareness that can make the difference between successfully staying out of debt and backsliding right into it. I started out this chapter suggesting you celebrate your success—because finishing the Fast is a major accomplishment. But I also hope that you'll see this stage in the process as an opportunity to really get a handle on what got you into debt in the first place. This clarity can help you stay focused and make permanent the positive changes you established. To get some insight on what you learned about yourself while on the Fast, ask yourself the following questions:

What was the hardest part of the Spending Fast?

Was there anything that I expected to be a challenge only to find it wasn't?

What part of the Fast made me the most proud? Bringing in new income? Slashing costs? Eliminating needs?

What am I most scared about now that the Spending Fast is over?

Did I discover any danger areas during the Fast? When was I the most tempted to spend money?

What did I learn about my relationships? Do I have friends that enable me to spend money when I know I shouldn't? How will I navigate those relationships now? *If you're single*: Will I look for financial well-being in a future partner?

Making Life Easier Will Cost Money

I know I've talked a lot about how little purchases add up to lots of money. And of course the opposite too: Cutting back on expenses whenever you can results in bigger savings than you would think. After the Fast, when I was reflecting on how I got into my financial mess in the first place, I realized that many of my little purchases were about "making life easier." An article in the *New York Post* told the story of a woman named Kris Ruby who had lost her credit card and borrowed her dad's. Kris's dad was shocked when he saw the bill: Kris had spent $225 in one week on *sushi*. She spent $11,000 on take-out in one year. Apparently she's not alone, because many other people with tough schedules talked about the ease of ordering take-out, even though it was costing some of them nearly as much as their rent.

While most people will not go as far as dropping five figures on take-out food, some really expensive habits sneak in when we choose to spend money to make life easier. I'm not talking about an occasional dinner out with friends or family—or a once-in-a-while pizza delivery. I'm talking about living life in a way that focuses on ease rather that practicality. I realize being practical might sound boring, but the bottom line is that spending $20 per meal three times a day (as one person mentioned in that article did) *isn't* ultimately making your life easier. It's a quick fix, and while you may not have to worry about grocery shopping, cooking, or cleaning up after a meal, you're going to have big problems from spending so much money on food, unless you're rolling in dough.

Obviously spending money to make life easier isn't limited to picking up take-out. There are countless ways to spend money under the guise of making life easier. That's how I felt each time I bought a new top: *Here's yet one more day I can go without doing laundry.*

Now that you've finished the Spending Fast and are transitioning into the Spending Diet, it's worth it to take the time to think about the sacrifices you made. It was worth it—you're either debt-free or closer to it. Nothing comes easy, and you've proven you can handle a lot. Don't slip back into debt by making easy choices. Organize your life in a way that enables you to do what you must without spending extra money. Convenience options are rarely cheaper, and the extra expense may not be worth it to you in the long run when you could be using that money to get out of debt. Here are some examples of excessive spending for convenience's sake:

Obviously, take-out food

That morning coffee and breakfast burrito

Paying for parking rather than driving around to look for a spot on the street

Dropping off shirts at the cleaners so you don't have to iron them

Paying a dog walker

Picking up milk at the 7-Eleven because it's on the way home and you don't want to drive or walk the extra few minutes to the store where it's cheaper

Having goods delivered to your house (diapers, groceries, toiletries, pet food)

Using a car service or cab instead of public transportation

Buying a new top or pants instead of mending what you have

Hiring someone to paint a room in your house

Paying to have someone cut your grass or do other landscaping

Buying lunch rather than packing it

Picking up food from drive-thrus on the way to or from work

Buying a smoothie or juice rather than making it yourself

Buying precut fruit or veggies

Buying frozen meals

Every time you're tempted to buy something to make life easier, take a moment to remind yourself how the opposite is really true. That purchase is delaying your debt-free life. What can you do to avoid these situations? Create a strategy you can put into place the next time you're tempted to spend money on something that allegedly makes life easier.

Danger Zone: The Slippery Slope of the Old Ways

I've already mentioned that I found the transition from Spending Fast to Spending Diet to be a rough one. I really needed the tough parameters of the Spending Fast to keep my spending in check. When my Fast ended and I basically released myself into the wild, I was a bit overwhelmed by my newfound freedom. Now that a decent amount of time has passed since my Spending Fast—and even my struggles with the Diet—I can tell you that there are some surefire signs that you're slipping to watch out for. I always make it a point to monitor my behavior when it comes to spending money, and if I see any of the following happen, I know I have to regroup and get myself back in check. Be sure to watch out for these behaviors, and note if any of them sound immediately familiar:

Signs You're Slipping Back to Your Old Ways

You have no idea how much money is in your checking account. You're ambivalent about finding out.

You're spending impulsively without taking that moment to pause. You're not stopping to think, *Do I have something like it at home?*, or *Can I get it cheaper elsewhere?*

You're not tracking your incoming and outgoing expenses.

You find yourself thinking, *I worked so hard. I deserve this.*

You're eating out more than you're eating in.

You go for the quick solution and decide it's easier to get something new rather than fix the item you already have.

You've lost your passion for saving money by spending less.

You slip up regularly and it doesn't bother you.

You let yourself think, *Hey, debt isn't so bad after all.*

Maybe you're still committed to your newfound financial health but you're starting to feel frustrated. Shame is like an evil ex who can make you feel so low that you end up doing something you'll regret later. Maybe you haven't fully gone back to your old ways, but you're close.

Be on Immediate Alert If . . .

You feel very discouraged.

You feel overwhelmed.

You're beating yourself up for not being "perfect."

You're not celebrating your successes and accomplishments.

You're focusing on the negative rather than the positive.

Staying out of debt for good means committing to the following ideas. Always and forever. This is your new financial code of ethics:

Spend less than you make.

Tell yourself no.

Find ways to make more money.

If you mess up, return what items you can, forgive yourself, and then continue on.

Stay committed; stay vigilant.

Return, Refocus, Recommit: The Three Rs Will Save You

Taking a quick trip back to your old, messy ways of handling money does not mean you're doomed. You haven't worked this hard and gotten this far only to give up and toss your dreams of being debt-free out the window. Be honest with yourself, and if you realize you're slipping or have really gone off the edge, dust yourself off and get back at it. The Three Rs:

Return: Take a quick look around—*What did I buy!!???* Return what you can ASAP. You'll feel better the second you send that package back or get the return credit at the store. Remember, if you can't get an actual cash refund or credit back on your card, get a gift card and hang on to it for Needs-Only spending.

Refocus: Home ownership! Quitting your job to freelance! Staying home with the baby! Exotic vacations! Whatever your goal is, remind yourself why you wanted to get out of debt in the first place and think about all the options that will open up for you when you do.

Recommit: You slipped, you're human. Don't beat yourself up over it, and don't give up on the Spending Fast over a mistake. Give yourself credit for everything you've accomplished, but also take the time to ponder why exactly you messed up. Were you bored and entertaining yourself with shopping? Did you not plan well and end up taking the easy (and costly) way out? Learn from what happened and move on.

What Are Your New Goals?

After the intensity of the Spending Fast, I knew I needed to set new goals for myself. When I started the Fast my goal was really basic: Get out of credit card debt. Throughout the course of the Fast, I added on: Pay off my student loan and my parents, and eventually be able to quit my courthouse job. Now that I knew I could handle the Spending Fast, I felt as if I could do anything. I had proof that I could set a challenging goal and accomplish it. So the question became *What else do I want to accomplish?* The goal of the Fast was so clear: Spend as little money as humanly possible so you can put more money toward your debt each month. I stuck to Needs-Only spending and watched the numbers grow on my Master Savings Sheet while my Debt Hit List dwindled down to almost nothing. I knew that I wanted to knock out the rest of my student loan (I had $5,693.21 to go)—and then what?

Setting Goals: Version 2.0

I had made so much progress during the Fast, but I wanted to make sure I would keep moving forward. I was inspired by my newfound ability to save, but the Spending Fast is not sustainable, and I needed to find a new place to draw inspiration. I realized that to keep myself on track, I needed to alter my focus. My life was no longer about going without to pay off a giant debt. I was able to see how my sacrifices (which felt a lot less like sacrifices at this point) could lead me to positive places.

The next questions were: *What do I want now? What do I want for my near and long-term future?* I started to think seriously about setting new goals. Keeping myself permanently on a Spending Diet seemed much more feasible when I had a prize in mind. The Spending Fast taught me I could meet my goal of getting out of debt, but I realized I needed to define exactly what it was I wanted if I was going to stay there. If you don't know that you want to own an apartment in New York City or take a month off to hike in South America, how are you going to stay focused and on track? Obviously your goals don't have to be about property or travel—you may simply want to save a year's worth of expenses in the bank or replace your ratty furniture. What you want is up to you.

In order to get a clear grasp on my new goals, I had to spend some time seriously thinking about what it was I wanted. You'll soon see, as I did, that once you're out of debt you have many more options available to you. I lived on far less money than I had pre–Spending Fast, so I could actually start thinking about how I wanted to live and not how I would be forced to live because my debt determined my choices. I considered my, and my husband's, long-term goals and what would be best for our family as a whole. The goals I started to focus on now that I wasn't saddled by debt were:

> Put money into and continue to build savings
> Think about investing in real estate
> Go part-time at the courthouse (start phasing out of the day job and phasing into full-time blogging, writing, and photography)
> Quit working at the courthouse and work from home full-time (continuing to build our photography business and write more)

Have a baby and be free to decide if Aaron or I would stay home with the
  baby
Continue to keep expenses low by living well within our means
Make enough from the photography business that Aaron can leave his day
  job if he wants
Be able to work from anywhere so we can travel (possibly in a tiny house?)

As with every big life event—getting out of debt, changing jobs, moving, getting married, having a baby—it's important to ask yourself if what you're doing financially is still working, and if you're leading yourself where you want to be in life. Post–Spending Fast is the perfect time to reevaluate your life goals. There's nothing sadder than clinging to something that's only *kind of* working because you're afraid of change. I'm talking the financial version of that boyfriend you were afraid to break up with. He was super-hot and funny, and though something felt *off* somehow, you were scared to let go. Trust me, it may not feel like it at the time, but you'll look back and be so thankful you let go of your old spending habits and opened your arms to this new way of life.

You've just shown you can take control of your money, which isn't easy. Now it's time to think about what you want to do with that money as more of it heads your way. Try the following exercises to get a really strong sense of your best next steps.

What Do You Want to Accomplish?

Write out a list of goals you want to accomplish. Again, if you don't know what you want, how are you going to get it? Define it to get it. Be as descriptive as possible when writing out your goals so that you can start to feel what it will be like when you reach them. Ideally, when you think about these accomplishments you should feel excitement, which will act as fuel to get you there. You can draw on this feeling for inspiration every day.

What Are the Substeps (The Little Steps Along the Way)?

You'll likely need to reach smaller goals along the road to a bigger one. Think about the substeps or subgoals that make up each main goal. Breaking a big goal into bite-sized pieces makes that ultimate goal easier to reach. Brain-blob the possible steps you'll need to take in order to make that goal a reality, then refine your list. It's entirely possible that your subgoals will have their own subgoals.

For example, let's say you've just gotten big news: You're pregnant! And you really want to stay home with the new baby. You'll definitely need to do some serious financial planning. Some of the steps you may need to make this goal a reality include *get out of debt* and *develop a new income stream*. Break down both of those subgoals into bite-sized actions. What steps would you need to take to develop a new income stream? Start freelancing again? Reach out to colleagues about freelance work? Design a digital flyer pitching your services? Make sure you cover every detail to make your goal reachable.

Create a To-Do List

To keep yourself on track, create a to-do list so you can check off steps and celebrate your progress as you move along. Decide what a logical first step would be and start there. Think about what you can accomplish next and so on, making a list of the various substeps you need to take to reach that goal. Keep your list where you can always see it—it's your map leading you directly to your goal.

Set a Time Frame

If you're giving yourself until the end of time to reach a goal, it's just not going to happen. Set a reasonable time frame, one that causes you to push yourself but is still realistic. In some instances, your time frame may be directly related to the situation. For instance, if it's your goal to be able to afford to live without roommates and your lease is up in six months, you clearly have a six-month window to reach that goal.

Hello, Savings

Many people freak out when they learn there is no savings component to the Spending Fast. As I said earlier, my goal was to get out of debt as soon as possible (and avoid paying additional interest and fees). Upon hitting the fifteenth month of paying off debt, I sent my last payment to my creditors! All $23,605.10 of my debt was gone! Now that my debt was behind me, I was all about stashing money away in savings. I'm not going to talk about the pros and cons of 401(k)s, CDs, real estate investments, or money market accounts. I do, though, definitely recommend you talk to your bank representative, a financial professional, or hell, your parents or a super-smart friend who works in finance to help you make some serious decisions about saving money. Just as the Spending Fast and the Spending Diet have to be tailored to your life to work ideally for you, saving money also requires that you find the best method possible *for you*.

The following ideas explain how to get in the habit of building a savings with that money you're no longer tossing toward your debt. These suggestions are methods that have worked for me:

> Put all your loose change and bills in a jar. Deposit it weekly or monthly into a savings account.
>
> Start an automatic withdrawal from your checking account to your savings account.
>
> Send yourself an invoice each month for a set amount. You can label it "Invoice: future home" or whatever your goal is to keep you focused and excited about saving.
>
> Sign up for "round up" at your bank. Some banks offer a service in which they round up your purchases to the next dollar, automatically putting those extra pennies into your savings account. For example, if you pay $42.10 for groceries, ninety cents will automatically be deposited into your savings account.

Tell yourself that if you spend $72 on nonessentials, you'll have to deposit
$72 into savings.

If you feel overwhelmed, focus on short-term savings goals, such as $100 a
week or even a few dollars a day. The "few dollars a day" method works
for many people because it's very manageable.

It doesn't matter how you choose to save as long as you welcome this super-healthy practice into your life. You've made it through your Spending Fast—and you feel amazing. Soon your savings account will be filling up, and your debt will be in your distant past.

I'm No Longer Part of the Problem

A couple of months ago my twin sister, Kelly, sent me an eight-word text that simply said: "Today is Day 1 of my Spending Fast." We're close, and we talk frequently about how her Spending Fast is going—I like to be there to cheer her on. I should add that my sister is doing her Fast while running her own business and raising three children on her own.

Recently, Kelly told me she'd received a $2,000 check in the mail. The month before she had received $4,000—and another hefty amount had arrived just a few weeks before that. Kelly had just gone through a divorce; a tax issue had been sorted out, and the mutual fund she shared with her ex-husband had been liquidated. We were talking about what good timing that was—how lucky she was that checks had started pouring in during her Spending Fast.

As we talked about it, I remembered that I'd had a similar experience after my Spending Fast had started. All of a sudden I was finding myself on the receiving end of money. I was wondering why this was happening. I thought, *If this had happened before the Spending Fast, I wouldn't have gotten into so much debt!* Looking back, I know that's not true. Had I not done the Fast, I would have found at least twenty different ways to spend that money.

I'd spent years telling myself that money was the biggest problem in my life. Now I thought differently. I was taking action. I was asking myself, *How can I make more money? What can I do to get out of debt faster?* I was now living the solution. When I finally stopped being a victim of my debt, I allowed the money to come into my life. I took responsibility for the choices I made, their resulting consequences, and I made my life change by taking action. I was no longer waiting for life to magically get better on its own. I was creating the answers instead of expecting them to come to me. I learned how to attract money rather than repel it, and I learned that getting out of debt was, more than anything, a belief in the future. I was trusting that by suffering through the Spending Fast in the present, I would set myself up for a stable future, and that's exactly what happened. It's not as if my sister and I are supernatural twins with the power to conjure money with the blink of an eye—we just stopped asking *Why?* and started asking *How?* We made the internal shift and took control of our money, and as a result changed the course of our lives. Who knows where it will take us? Who knows where it will take *you?*

Debt no longer has the power to threaten the life you were meant to live. You have the power. You are the solution.

151 THINGS TO DO INSTEAD of SPENDING MONEY

1. Read the archives of your favorite blogs.
2. Build a fort.
3. Actually make the projects from your Pinterest pins.
4. Explore recipes online or in your cookbooks and vow to be creative with your meals.
5. Mend the clothes that need mending.
6. Watch every Netflix movie that your favorite actor or actress is in.
7. Use your gift certificates!
8. Get organized. Go through all those old papers, clean up your computer's hard drive, find a home for any errant items in your house.
9. Cut your own hair.
10. Try out some new hairstyles.
11. Have a spa day at home!
12. Take a picture an hour.
13. Write old-school paper letters.
14. Make gifts!
15. Tackle a task that's been on your mind.
16. Declutter.
17. Deep-clean your house from top to bottom.

18. Clean your car.
19. Get rid of all the items in your closet and dresser that you don't absolutely love.
20. Throw a potluck.
21. Rearrange your furniture.
22. Volunteer.
23. Enjoy free library and community events.
24. Catch up on your reading.
25. Sleep in.
26. Take a nap.
27. Go for a run.
28. Peruse magazines at a bookstore.
29. Go Dumpster-diving!
30. Call your international relatives (use a free Internet service such as Skype).
31. Organize your print and digital photos.
32. Make homemade cards.
33. Make cookies.
34. Update your to-do list.
35. Write a story and jot down memories.
36. Start a Happy Book by compiling all your good memories in one place.
37. See your city in a new way by going on a bike ride.
38. Hike.
39. See if you can return anything you've bought.
40. Wash all your linens.
41. Take inventory of your finances and see where you can make some changes.
42. Create three short-term goals, three one-year goals, three five-year goals, and three ten-year goals.
43. Write down twenty things that you're grateful for right this minute.
44. Have a sleepover.
45. Make meaningful contact. Tell the people in your life why they're important to you.
46. Have your friends over to just hang out.

47. Hop on the bus and take a route you normally don't take.

48. Go to an open mic night.

49. Take advantage of the free week offer at a new gym or yoga studio.

50. Put your unused items on Craigslist.

51. Sell your unwanted items to a pawnshop.

52. Organize a clothing or accessories swap.

53. Hold a yard sale.

54. Donate to the thrift store.

55. Connect with an old friend.

56. Be anonymously nice. (Take a look at the list *134 Random Acts of Kindness* on AndThenWeSaved.com for inspiration and ideas.)

57. Tweeze your eyebrows.

58. Memorize all the US presidents in order.

59. Rerecord your voice-mail message.

60. Help a friend move.

61. Clean your mirrors, and when you're done wash the windows, and then come over to my house and do mine.

62. Polish your shoes.

63. Clean those filthy blinds.

64. Write out a secret you've never told anyone before. You know the deepest, darkest one? Yeah, that one. Write it down and then burn the paper.

65. Write a letter to someone who passed away.

66. Organize your holiday decorations.

67. Bleed your radiator.

68. Refill all the hand soaps in your home.

69. Drink a glass of water.

70. Stretch and breathe deeply.

71. Take out your recycling.

72. Fly a kite.

73. Water your plants.

74. Pet your cat or dog (or your neighbor's cats and dogs).

75. Write a packing list for an upcoming trip.

76. Clean all the crap out of your junk drawer.

77. Knit or crochet a scarf. Don't know how to knit or crochet? This is the perfect time to learn.

78. Polish your silver and sharpen your knives.

79. Go through all your old pens and markers. Test them out and throw out the ones that don't work anymore.

80. Print off a coloring page from the Internet and color it in. It's surprisingly fun.

81. Be present. Where are you? What are you doing? What sounds do you hear around you? What does your breathing sound and feel like? How does the weight of your body feel?

82. Have a staring contest, then an arm-wrestling competition.

83. Wash your car.

84. Go to a Debtors Anonymous meeting.

85. Reach out to new business contacts and leads.

86. Swim laps at a local pool.

87. Look at your old school yearbooks.

88. Organize your purse, wallet, backpack, or all three.

89. Spackle the holes in your walls.

90. If you're spiritual, write a prayer.

91. Go through your socks and get rid of the ones without matches.

92. Update your résumé/curriculum vitae.

93. Babysit.

94. Visit the elderly at a nursing home.

95. Perfect your Candy Crush game.

96. Go geocaching.

97. Prep your taxes.

98. Talk to your neighbor.

99. Read the Missed Connections section on Craigslist, and when you're done with that, read the site's "Best of" section.

100. Go through old e-mails and letters from former lovers to see how different you are now from then.

101. Write your memoir.

102. Warning: This one is depressing. Write your own eulogy or obituary.

103. Learn a language from CDs from the library or use the Duolingo website or app (Duolingo is a free, crowdsourced language-learning platform).

104. Hunt down a better homeowner's insurance policy rate.

105. Make up or search out some recipes using potatoes, eggs, and oatmeal so you can have new cheap, go-to meal staples.

106. Study up on how to coupon really well, and then seek out coupons.

107. Plan out your meals for the upcoming month.

108. Go out and collect cans to turn in for money. (This applies only to certain states.)

109. Clean up some graffiti or litter around town.

110. Catch fireflies.

111. Check out some new music from your library.

112. Lie on the grass, look up at the clouds, and decide what animals the clouds look like.

113. Borrow e-books from your local library.

114. Switch to a credit union for your banking.

115. Decide on your best physical feature and your best personality trait.

116. Think up future pet or kid names.

117. Write a letter to your future or existing kid(s).

118. Write your future self a letter.

119. Take the Get Out of Debt Pledge on AndThenWeSaved.com.

120. Upcycle your clothes.

121. Repaint your furniture with paint you already own, or get a gallon of discounted, "mis-tinted" paint from your local hardware store.

122. Decorate a ceramic mug with a permanent marker, and then bake it so the ink sets (250°F for 2 hours).

123. Cute-ify your house by making bunting out of scrap pieces of card stock, fabric, or yarn.

124. Plan a dream trip (even if you never take the trip, it's still fun to dream!).

125. Pull a Forrest Gump and see how far you can run. If you get to another state, turn around.

126. See how many compliments you can give out at work without seeming like a suck-up.

127. Ask a coworker if he or she needs help with anything.
128. Write a letter to the editor of your local paper.
129. Come up with your own list of things to do instead of spending money and then e-mail them to me so I can do them too.
130. Make an origami paper crane.
131. Learn a magic trick.
132. Make a Wants and Needs List.
133. Pretend you're a comedian and create a stand-up routine.
134. Say hi to everyone you encounter.
135. Draw yourself as a vampire or zombie. And when you're done with that, draw your friends as vampires or zombies.
136. Have a YouTube night and watch prank, parkour, or kitten videos.
137. Cancel your cable service.
138. Start up a conversation with a stranger.
139. Teach yourself how to make a ringtone and install it on your phone.
140. Create a list of movies you want to see. Check each one out of the library, marking off your list as you go.
141. Have an impromptu dance party.
142. Call someone who may be lonely.
143. Right a wrong.
144. Forgive yourself and others for mistakes that have been made. Let any grudges go.
145. Ride on the back of a motorcycle.
146. Make a list of places to visit.
147. Make a list of twenty-nine things to do before you're twenty-nine (or whatever age you'll be turning next).
148. Start (and keep) a journal.
149. Start a dream diary. Look up and interpret the meaning of your dreams.
150. Listen to a podcast or record one of your own.
151. Have a nineties movie marathon, complete with side ponytails and lots of neon.

ACKNOWLEDGMENTS

Thank you to the people without whose contributions and support this book could not have been written: my cowriter, Paula Balzer, who ended up putting way more time and energy into this project than planned, and who tirelessly worked on it until the very end. Thank you to my incredible publisher, Cassie Jones; to Kara Zauberman; and to the entire team at William Morrow for believing in this book and for patiently guiding me through the publishing process. Thank you to my literary agent, Jenny Bent, who is unfailingly honest and believed in this book from the very beginning. Thank you to Amy Haimerl, who first dubbed me a "debt-buster" on *CNNMoney*, which showed my site to a national audience and set the excitement for AndThenWeSaved .com in motion. Thank you to my parents, Frank and Carol Newell; my siblings, Kelly, Christine, and Jim; and my friends, especially Shayla Pauley, for constantly cheering me along and for always being forthright and honest when I asked for their opinions. Thank you to my former boss, Judge William Robbins, for teaching me the power of adaptability and for allowing me to work part-time so I could pursue my higher purpose in life. Thank you also to my funny and gorgeous husband, Aaron Jones, who supports and loves me even when I'm hungry and tired. I'm so glad I get to live my life with you and sweet Henry. Lastly, thank you most of all to the readers of AndThen WeSaved.com. Your determination and persistence is mind-blowing and so incredibly inspiring. You have taken the Spending Fast and the Spending Diet to levels I never dreamed were possible.

REFERENCES: WORKS CITED

Akers, Elizabeth J., and Matthew M. Chingos. *Are College Students Borrowing Blindly?* Brown Center on Education Policy at the Brookings Institution. December 2014. http://www.brookings.edu/~/media/research/files/reports/2014/12/10%20borrowing%20blindly/are%20college%20students%20borrowing%20blindly_dec%202014.pdf.

Bidwell, Allie. "Student Loan Default Rate Drops 7 Percent in One Year." *U.S. News & World Report*. September 24, 2014. http://www.usnews.com/news/articles/2014/09/24/student-loan-default-rate-decreases-but-some-question-federal-free-passes.

Bijleveld, Erik, and Henk Aarts, eds. *The Psychological Science of Money*. New York: Springer-Verlag, 2014.

Chen, Tim. "American Household Credit Card Debt Statistics: 2015." *NerdWallet Credit Card* (blog). 2015. https://www.nerdwallet.com/blog/credit-card-data/average-credit-card-debt-household.

Cho, Janet H. "Holiday Shopping Ticked Up 4% to $616.1 Billion in November and December 2014, National Retail Federation Says." *Plain Dealer*. January 14, 2015. http://www.cleveland.com/business/index.ssf/2015/01/holiday_shopping_ticked_up_4_t.html.

Ellis, Blake. "One in Ten Unemployed Denied Jobs Due to Credit Checks." *CNNMoney*. March 14, 2013. http://money.cnn.com/2013/03/04/pf/employer-credit-checks/.

Federal Trade Commission. "Consumer Information." *Disputing Errors on Credit Reports*. March 2014. http://www.consumer.ftc.gov/articles/0151-disputing-errors-credit-reports.

Green, Penelope. "Kissing Your Socks Goodbye." *New York Times*. October 22, 2014. http://www.nytimes.com/2014/10/23/garden/home-organization-advice-from-marie-kondo.html?_r=0.

Gunnars, Kris. "How Much Water Should You Drink Per Day?" *Authority Nutrition*. October 24, 2013. http://authoritynutrition.com/how-much-water-should-you-drink-per-day/.

Hanna, Holly Reisem. "27 Things You Can Sell from Home to Make Money." *The Work at Home Woman RSS* (blog). http://www.theworkathomewoman.com/things-to-sell/.

Harvard Health Publications. "In Praise of Gratitude." November 1, 2011. http://www.health.harvard.edu/newsletter_article/in-praise-of-gratitude.

Hefling, Kimberly. "Gov. Report Shows Seniors Owe $18 Billion in Student Loan Debt." The Rundown. *PBS NewsHour*. September 10, 2014. http://www.pbs.org/newshour/rundown/seniors-owe-18-billion-student-loan-debt/.

Hiken, Melanie. "Average Wedding Bill Hits $30,000." *CNNMoney*. March 28, 2014. http://money.cnn.com/2014/03/28/pf/average-wedding-cost/index.html.

Jaude, Karim. "How to Set and Attain Goals for Success." *Power to Change: How to Set and Attain Goals for Success Comments*. 2004. http://powertochange.com/world/setattaingoals/.

Loewenstein, George. "Anticipation and the Valuation of Delayed Consumption." *The Economic Journal* 97, no. 387 (1987): 666–84. http://www.cmu.edu/dietrich/sds/docs/loewenstein/AnticipationDelayed.pdf.

Richins, Marsha L. "When Wanting Is Better Than Having: Materialism, Transformation Expectations, and Product-Evoked Emotions in the Purchase Process." *Journal of Consumer Research*. June 2013. http://www.press.uchicago.edu/pressReleases/2013/January/jcr1301Richins.html

Taft, Michael W. "Five Ways Our Need to Fit In Controls Us." *Science 2.0*. March 14, 2012. http://www.science20.com/michael_taft/five_ways_our_need_fit_controls_us-87994.

Touryalai, Halah. "$1 Trillion Student Loan Problem Keeps Getting Worse." *Forbes*. February 21, 2014. http://www.forbes.com/sites/halahtouryalai/2014/02/21/1-trillion-student-loan-problem-keeps-getting-worse/.

Williams, Alex. "Saying No to College." *New York Times*. December 1, 2012. http://www.nytimes.com/2012/12/02/fashion/saying-no-to-college.html.

Wong, Kristin. "What to Do When You Can't Afford to Pay Your Student Loans." *Two Cents*. June 27, 2014. http://twocents.lifehacker.com/what-to-do-when-you-cant-afford-to-pay-your-student-loa-1594957967.

INDEX

reevaluating needs on, 197
referring to frequently, 82
staying on track with, 78
wedding dresses, selling, 166
wedding expenses, 9–10
wedding photography, 146–47
weight loss, 193
Wi-Fi access, 84
window shopping, 90
WordPress, 73

Y

yard sales
classic, 162–66
virtual, 166–68
yoga, 88
YouTube, 33

Z

Zuckerberg, Mark, 125